W0010290

To

_____

From

_____

Date

_____

Visit Christian Art Gifts website at www.christianartgifts.com.

One Minute with God for Students

Published by Christian Art Gifts, Inc.

Previously published as The One Year Mini for Students.
First printing by Tyndale House Publishers, in 2006.

Designed by Alyssa Montalto

General editors: Ronald A. Beers, Linda Taylor

Contributing editors: Rebecca Beers, Amy Mason, Christopher Mason. Contributing
writers: V. Gilbert Beers, Ronald A. Beers, Brian R. Coffey, Jonathan Farrar, Jonathan
Gray, Shawn A. Harrison, Sandy Hull, Rhonda K. O'Brien, Douglas J. Rumford.

ISBN: 978-1-64272-844-6

Printed in China

26 25 24 23 22 21
10 9 8 7 6 5 4 3 2 1

ONE MINUTE
-- WITH --
GOD
FOR
STUDENTS
-- 365 --
DAILY DEVOTIONS

Christian art gifts

January

Q Everyone is making New Year's resolutions.
What kinds of resolutions should I set for myself?

God's Response

For even the Son of Man came not to be served but to serve others and to give His life as a ransom for many. - Mark 10:45

Let love be your highest goal! - 1 Corinthians 14:1

I brought glory to You here on earth by completing the work You gave Me to do. - John 17:4

Everyone may make New Year's resolutions, but few people actually keep them. In fact, most people break their resolutions within three months. Rather than making a long list of things you hope to do this year, focus on the one thing that really matters—a daily resolution to be like Jesus. While He was on earth, Jesus loved, served, and gave glory to God. When you resolve to live that way, you will find that every day brings a new adventure. Decide today to be more like Jesus this year by loving and serving God and others, and by bringing glory to God in the way you live.

This Is Promising

Our goal is to please Him. - 2 Corinthians 5:9

Q

What life goals will bring me closer to God?

God's Response

Are you seeking great things for yourself? Don't do it! - Jeremiah 45:5

If you want to be a friend of the world, you make yourself an enemy of God. - James 4:4

Enoch lived 365 years, walking in close fellowship with God. Then one day he disappeared, because God took him. - Genesis 5:23-24

Have you ever set a goal for yourself? Did you reach it? Why or why not? The kinds of goals you set should help you develop a better relationship with God. That means focusing on God and on His direction for your life, not on seeking only pleasure or great things for yourself. The Bible says that Enoch had a great relationship with God for 365 years! Why not walk with God for the next 365 days? What would it take for you to reach this goal?

This Is Promising

Love the LORD your God, walk in all His ways, obey His commands, hold firmly to Him, and serve Him with all your heart and all your soul. - Joshua 22:5

Q Last year I made some mistakes.
How can I avoid making them again?

God's Response

I focus on this one thing: Forgetting the past and looking forward to what lies ahead … - Philippians 3:13

And I am certain that God, Who began the good work within you, will continue His work until it is finally finished on the day when Christ Jesus returns. - Philippians 1:6

There can be a big difference between making a mistake and committing a sin. A mistake is getting the wrong answer on a test. A sin is cheating in order to get a better grade. You can often avoid repeating a mistake by studying harder, planning better, or double-checking your work. But to avoid repeating the same sin, you need God's help. The regret you feel over a sin indicates that you want to be different, and that desire is from God. Ask God to help you be different!

This Is Promising

Great is His faithfulness; His mercies begin afresh each morning.
- Lamentations 3:23

Q

How can I make better choices this year than I did last year?

God's Response

When Jesus came by, He looked up at Zacchaeus and called him by name. "Zacchaeus!" He said. "Quick, come down! I must be a guest in your home today." Zacchaeus quickly climbed down and took Jesus to his house in great excitement and joy. But the people were displeased. "He has gone to be the guest of a notorious sinner," they grumbled. Meanwhile, Zacchaeus stood before the Lord and said, "I will give half my wealth to the poor, Lord, and if I have cheated people on their taxes, I will give them back four times as much!" - Luke 19:5-8

Zacchaeus had clearly made some bad choices—the people in the crowd called him a "notorious sinner." But after Jesus spent some time with him, Zacchaeus's life changed, and he wanted to make better choices. Our choices reflect the kind of people we are, and this is often influenced by whom we spend time with. Zacchaeus began to change when he spent time with Jesus. That is the best choice you can make too!

This Is Promising

You can make this choice by loving the LORD your God, obeying Him, and committing yourself firmly to Him.- Deuteronomy 30:20

Q

Will God tell me if I'm making the right choices?

God's Response

I appeal to you to show kindness to my child, Onesimus. I became his father in the faith while here in prison. Onesimus hasn't been of much use to you in the past, but now he is very useful to both of us. I am sending him back to you, and with him comes my own heart.... He is no longer like a slave to you. He is more than a slave, for he is a beloved brother.
- Philemon 1:10-12, 16

Why are the right choices often the hardest ones to make? It would not be easy for Onesimus to return to the master from whom he had stolen money and run away. Onesimus's owner, Philemon, had to decide whether to take his runaway slave back as a fellow believer. Paul advised both men to make the right choices. When you know the right thing to do, God will confirm it deep in your heart, and other trusted people around you will agree with it. It may not make it easier, but knowing what is right can give you the courage to do it. The Bible calls this wisdom, which comes from the Word of God.

This Is Promising

Joyful is the person who finds wisdom, the one who gains understanding.
- Proverbs 3:13

What happens when I mess up?

God's Response

Hanani, one of my brothers, came to visit me with some other men who had just arrived from Judah. I asked them about the Jews who had returned there from captivity and about how things were going in Jerusalem. They said to me, "Things are not going well for those who returned to the province of Judah. They are in great trouble and disgrace. The wall of Jerusalem has been torn down, and the gates have been destroyed by fire." - Nehemiah 1:2-3

The people of Israel had messed up—badly. In fact, God punished them by sending them off in captivity to a foreign land and allowing their beloved city of Jerusalem to be destroyed. But God gives second chances. He sent a leader named Nehemiah to provide the plan and the encouragement to help the people rebuild the wall of their city. When you mess up, expect to face the consequences and ask God to help you start again. He is the God of second chances.

This Is Promising

"Yes, let's rebuild the wall!" So they began the good work. - Nehemiah 2:18

Q

What if I keep messing up? Will God ever stop forgiving me? Can I sin too much or too often?

God's Response

Jacob took the food to his father. "My father?" he said. "Yes, my son," Isaac answered. "Who are you—Esau or Jacob?" Jacob replied, "It's Esau, your firstborn son. I've done as you told me. Here is the wild game. Now sit up and eat it so you can give me your blessing." - Genesis 27:18-19

Jacob made many mistakes in his life—it seems he was always deceiving someone. He faced the consequences of his sins and received God's forgiveness. God did not abandon Jacob even when he repeatedly acted in selfish and deceitful ways. Your life will never be 100 percent sin-free, but God will not give up on you, however many times you mess up. The bottom line is that God is faithful even when we are not.

This Is Promising

I am certain that God, Who began the good work within you, will continue His work until it is finally finished on the day when Christ Jesus returns.
- Philippians 1:6

Q If God's will is going to happen anyway, do my choices really matter?

God's Response

The LORD said to Moses, "Why are you crying out to Me? Tell the people to get moving!" - Exodus 14:15

Seek His will in all you do, and He will show you which path to take.
- Proverbs 3:6

You are not irrelevant—your choices make a difference. You can choose whether or not to participate in God's plan. God's work will get done—if not by you, then by someone else. If you want to participate in God's will, you can't sit around waiting for Him to write a message on the wall. Seek His guidance, and then make a decision to move ahead. If you always ask God for guidance, your choices will usually be in line with His intentions, and you will be involved in His work.

This Is Promising

You guide me with Your counsel, leading me to a glorious destiny.
- Psalm 73:24

Q   Will God forgive me for the dumb things
         I've done?

God's Response

Though your sins are like scarlet, I will make them as white as snow.
Though they are red like crimson, I will make them as white as wool.
- Isaiah 1:18

O Lord, You are so good, so ready to forgive, so full of unfailing love for all
who ask for Your help. - Psalm 86:5

Forgiveness requires two parties—one to ask for it and the other to give it. Between you and God, you are always on the asking side and He is always on the giving side. Fortunately, if you are sincere, you are assured of God's forgiveness. No matter what mistakes you've made, God promises that He will take the stain of your sins and make it "white as snow."

This Is Promising

He forgives all my sins and heals all my diseases. - Psalm 103:3

Q How can I get over the stupid things
I've said or done?

God's Response

*If we confess our sins to Him, he is faithful and just to forgive us our sins
and to cleanse us from all wickedness.* - 1 John 1:9

You are holy and blameless as you stand before Him without a single fault.
- Colossians 1:22

Sometimes forgiving yourself is the hardest thing to do, usually
because you feel guilty or you realize how deeply you have hurt
someone. The Bible says that when you confess your sin to Jesus, He
forgives you totally and completely. He looks at you as though you
had never sinned. You will still have to deal with the consequences
that your sin has set in motion, but as far as God is concerned, your
heart is clean and you're ready for a fresh start. When you forgive
yourself as Jesus has forgiven you, you will experience the joy and
freedom God wants to give you.

This Is Promising

He has removed our sins as far from us as the east is from the west.
- Psalm 103:12

Q Are any sins too big to be forgiven?

God's Response

Manasseh also sacrificed his own sons in the fire in the valley of Ben-Hinnom. He practiced sorcery, divination, and witchcraft, and he consulted with mediums and psychics. - 2 Chronicles 33:6

While in deep distress, Manasseh sought the LORD his God and sincerely humbled himself before the God of his ancestors. And when he prayed, the LORD listened to him and was moved by his request. - 2 Chronicles 33:12-13

When it comes to the all-time big-sin list, King Manasseh has got to be near the top. He was one of the most evil kings we read about in the Old Testament. Yet when he sincerely called out to God for help, no sin was too big for God to forgive. Jesus' sacrifice on the cross is powerful enough to cover any sin. Like Manasseh, you must humble yourself, be courageous, and ask for forgiveness.

This Is Promising

This is My blood.... It is poured out as a sacrifice to forgive the sins of many. - Matthew 26:28

Q

I have some big decisions to make this year. Will God show me the right direction to take?

God's Response

Gideon said to God, "If you are truly going to use me to rescue Israel as You promised, prove it to me in this way. I will put a wool fleece on the threshing floor tonight. If the fleece is wet with dew in the morning but the ground is dry, then I will know that You are going to help me rescue Israel as You promised." - Judges 6:36-37

Have you ever asked God for a sign? Gideon had to decide whether or not he would believe God's promise of victory, so he put out a fleece and asked God to make a miracle happen. God complied, but this is not usually the way to make big decisions. Our greatest means of God's guidance is His Word, the Bible. Unlike Gideon, you have God's complete, revealed Word. If you want God to guide you, don't ask for signs, but study the Bible. God won't try to make His will a puzzle to you; He just wants you to listen for His guidance and then move ahead when He shows you the way.

This Is Promising

If you need wisdom, ask our generous God, and He will give it to you.
- James 1:5

Q

Does each decision I make really matter that much?

God's Response

Commit your actions to the LORD, and your plans will succeed.
- Proverbs 16:3

Oh, that we might know the LORD! Let us press on to know Him. He will respond to us as surely as the arrival of dawn or the coming of rains in early spring. - Hosea 6:3

Making right decisions is like hiking; each step puts you a little farther down the path. Sometimes the right decision is simply being faithful in little things. God's will for you today is to obey Him, serve others, read His Word, and do what is right. If you stay in the center of His will today, you can be sure that you will be in the center of His will twenty years from now. When you have been faithful over time, there comes a point where it feels that God is letting you choose which way to go. What is really happening is that you are close enough to God to recognize His leading in your life.

This Is Promising

My steps have stayed on Your path; I have not wavered from following You. - Psalm 17:5

Q Are there certain steps to take for making good decisions?

God's Response

Your laws please me; they give me wise advice. - Psalm 119:24

Jesus went up on a mountain to pray, and He prayed to God all night. - Luke 6:12

There is safety in having many advisers. - Proverbs 11:14

Do you ever feel afraid of making the wrong decision? God is not waiting for you to make the wrong decision so that He can zap you. He wants to help you make the right choices. A right decision will be consistent with the principles of truth found in God's Word. If there is only one option that will please God, then that is the right decision. Pray for guidance and get wise advice from other Christians. If you find yourself with several options that are consistent with God's Word, then trust God to help you make the most of the path you choose.

This Is Promising

Your commands make me wiser than my enemies, for they are my constant guide. - Psalm 119:98

Q

Will God tell me what He wants me to do for the rest of my life?

God's Response

Your word is a lamp to guide my feet and a light for my path.
- Psalm 119:105

The LORD says, "I will guide you along the best pathway for your life. I will advise you and watch over you." - Psalm 32:8

Trust in the LORD with all your heart; do not depend on your own understanding. - Proverbs 3:5

If we saw too much of the future, we'd either be very afraid of the bad things ahead or get very cocky about our accomplishments. God's guidance is less like a searchlight brightening a huge area and more like a flashlight shining on just enough of the path ahead to show you how to take the next few steps. God has a definite plan for you, but He usually doesn't reveal it all at once. He wants you to trust Him each step of the way.

This Is Promising

The LORD will work out His plans for my life—for Your faithful love, O LORD, endures forever. - Psalm 138:8

Q Does God really have a plan for my life?
Do I have a say about it?

God's Response

"I knew you before I formed you in your mother's womb. Before you were born I set you apart." ... "O Sovereign LORD," I said, "I can't speak for You! I'm too young!" The LORD replied, "Don't say, 'I'm too young,' for you must go wherever I send you and say whatever I tell you." - Jeremiah 1:5-7

God created you for a purpose. It only makes sense that He should know what will satisfy the longings of your heart. You have a "say" in that you can follow God and do what He already knows will fulfill you and make a difference for His Kingdom, or you can choose to go your own way. How much better to seek God's plan for you and follow it! Then you'll be sure that your life will have meaning and you will accomplish what God created you to do.

This Is Promising

You see me when I travel and when I rest at home. You know everything I do. - Psalm 139:3

Q Does God give me talents and abilities for a reason?

God's Response

Then the LORD said to Moses, "Look, I have specifically chosen Bezalel son of Uri, grandson of Hur, of the tribe of Judah. I have filled him with the Spirit of God, giving him great wisdom, ability, and expertise in all kinds of crafts. He is a master craftsman, expert in working with gold, silver, and bronze. He is skilled in engraving and mounting gemstones and in carving wood. He is a master at every craft!" - Exodus 31:1-5

Your talents and abilities are not random or accidental; they are part of the way that God has uniquely designed you. God gave Bezalel talent as a craftsman and commissioned him to create beautiful objects for the Tabernacle. God does His work on earth through people, so He gives each person special gifts and talents. Every ability you have is useful to God, so use each one for Him. What talents has God given you? These abilities may become your full-time job, or they may simply be hobbies. Either way, God can use them to accomplish His purposes. It is exciting and deeply satisfying to do the things you enjoy for God's service.

This Is Promising

God works in different ways, but it is the same God Who does the work in all of us. - 1 Corinthians 12:6

Q Does God show me what He wants me to do with my life by what I'm good at?

God's Response

[Potiphar] took Joseph and threw him into the prison.... Before long, the warden put Joseph in charge of all the other prisoners and over everything that happened in the prison. The warden had no more worries, because Joseph took care of everything. - Genesis 39:20-23

What do you want to do with your life? This is a tough question. You may find your first clues by considering your talents and abilities. While you may not get the perfect job that uses all of your skills, you can hopefully move into a career in which you work well because you are doing what you love to do. Sometimes, however, you will need to take a job because you need it, and trust that in the future, God will make use of whatever you learn there. God will not waste your time. Like Joseph, you should do the best you can with the job at hand. God will do the rest.

This Is Promising

Well done, my good and faithful servant. You have been faithful in handling this small amount, so now I will give you many more responsibilities.
- Matthew 25:21

My friendships are really important to me.
How can I make better friends?

God's Response

[David] met Jonathan, the king's son. There was an immediate bond of love between them, and they became the best of friends.... Jonathan made a solemn pact with David, because he loved him as he loved himself. Jonathan sealed the pact by taking off his robe and giving it to David, together with his tunic, sword, bow, and belt. - 1 Samuel 18:1-4

When David and Jonathan met, they became close friends at once. Their friendship is one of the deepest and closest recorded in the Bible, which is odd when you consider that Jonathan was the king's son (and in line for the throne) and David had been anointed to eventually become king. Jonathan knew this, but he and David were still best friends. They based their friendship on a common commitment to honor God; they let nothing come between them, they drew closer together when their friendship was tested, and they remained friends to the end. These are the marks of a true friend.

This Is Promising

A friend is always loyal. - Proverbs 17:17

Q

Lots of my friends aren't Christians.
Is that okay?

God's Response

Levi held a banquet in his home with Jesus as the guest of honor. Many of Levi's fellow tax collectors and other guests also ate with them. But the Pharisees and their teachers of religious law complained bitterly to Jesus' disciples, "Why do you eat and drink with such scum?" - Luke 5:29-30

It's not only okay to have non-Christian friends—it's good. Of course, it's also good to have Christian friends, because you need fellow believers to help you grow in your walk with God. Still, God has given you non-Christian friends for a reason. Like Levi (Matthew), you may be able to introduce them to Jesus. Just make sure that you don't compromise your faith when you're with those friends. Live as a follower of Jesus before them and trust that the things you say and the way you act will make them want to learn more about your faith.

This Is Promising

Jesus answered them, "Healthy people don't need a doctor—sick people do. I have come to call not those who think they are righteous, but those who know they are sinners and need to repent." - Luke 5:31-32

Q

What shall I do if some of my non-Christian friends have a bad influence on me?

God's Response

When you crossed the Jordan River and came to Jericho, the men of Jericho fought against you, as did the Amorites, the Perizzites, the Canaanites, the Hittites, the Girgashites, the Hivites, and the Jebusites. But I gave you victory over them.... Choose today whom you will serve. Would you prefer the gods your ancestors served beyond the Euphrates? Or will it be the gods of the Amorites in whose land you now live? But as for me and my family, we will serve the LORD. - Joshua 24:11, 15

If you find that you do things you know are wrong when you are with your non-Christian friends, then you must decide whether your first loyalty lies with your friends or with God. The choice is yours. By asking the question, you already know that your friends' influence is bad and will lead you away from God. Joshua understood that. Choosing God may mean deciding not to hang out with those friends, sharing this struggle with a Christian friend, or confronting a non-Christian friend with your concerns. Whatever you decide, stay true to God and do not turn away from Him.

This Is Promising

Choose life, so that you and your descendants might live! You can make this choice by loving the LORD your God, obeying Him, and committing yourself firmly to Him. This is the key to your life. - Deuteronomy 30:19-20

Q

What if the Christians I know are really weird?
Do I have to hang out with them?

God's Response

*God said to Noah, ... "Build a large boat.... I am about to cover the earth
with a flood."* - Genesis 6:13-14, 17

*"Don't be afraid, Mary," the angel told her.... "You will conceive and give
birth to a son." ... Mary asked the angel, "But how can this happen?
I am a virgin." The angel replied, "The Holy Spirit will come upon you."*
- Luke 1:30-31, 34-35

A man built a boat in the desert. A woman said that she was
pregnant—not from a man, but from the Holy Spirit. That's
pretty weird, yet the Bible calls Noah and Mary two of God's
favorite people. Many people who encountered Jesus considered
Him odd. All of us are a little weird, when you think about it. If you
follow Jesus, some people will think you are weird, and you will be
around people who others think are weird. Would you hang out
with someone even if he or she was weird? Jesus did that—He did
what was right without worrying about how it looked. When you
look beyond appearances and into a person's heart, you will see
someone that God values and loves. If God finds great value there,
so will you—if you look.

This Is Promising

*I have never turned away a stranger but have opened my doors to
everyone.* - Job 31:32

Q How can I be friends with certain people if
I know it will mean losing other friends?

God's Response

My friends laugh at me, for I call on God and expect an answer.
I am a just and blameless man, yet they laugh at me. - Job 12:4

My close friends detest me. Those I loved have turned against me.
- Job 19:19

What you're really asking is, "If I seek out Christian friends—or
hang out with the weird ones—I'm going to lose my non-Christian
friends. They're going to write me off as a freak." This may happen,
and the really sad part will be realizing that they weren't such good
friends after all. It hurts to have people turn their backs on you.
Your job is to continue to love them even when they reject you. It's
a tough job, but that's what Jesus has done for you!

This Is Promising

I once thought these things were valuable, but now I consider them
worthless because of what Christ has done. - Philippians 3:7

Q How can I have a good reputation?

God's Response

Noah was a righteous man, the only blameless person living on earth at the time, and he walked in close fellowship with God. - Genesis 6:9

Like it or not, you already have a reputation. Whether you intentionally try to project a certain image or could care less what others think, people do form an opinion of you based on what you do and say. You can't control what others think about you. The only reputation that really matters is what God thinks about you. The great thing about being a Christian is that God already loves you and thinks the world of you. You can't impress Him or make Him think any more of you, but you can have a growing relationship with Him!

This Is Promising

Choose a good reputation over great riches; being held in high esteem is better than silver or gold. - Proverbs 22:1

Q How can my friends know they can trust me?

God's Response

"If I die, treat my family with this faithful love, even when the LORD destroys all your enemies from the face of the earth." So Jonathan made a solemn pact with David. - 1 Samuel 20:14-16

His name was Mephibosheth; he was Jonathan's son and Saul's grandson. When he came to David, he bowed low to the ground in deep respect. David said, "Greetings, Mephibosheth." Mephibosheth replied, "I am your servant." "Don't be afraid!" David said. "I intend to show kindness to you because of my promise to your father, Jonathan." - 2 Samuel 9:6-7

Your friends will know they can trust you when you prove to be trustworthy. It's as simple as that. When a man became king in ancient days, it was common to kill off the entire family of the preceding king, but David promised he wouldn't do that. Even though Mephibosheth was the grandson of the previous king—and thus a potential threat—David cared for him like a son. When you keep your promises, people learn that they can trust you and you build a reputation for trustworthiness.

This Is Promising

A gossip goes around telling secrets, but those who are trustworthy can keep a confidence. - Proverbs 11:13

Q My two best friends are in an argument. What can I do to help?

God's Response

Now I appeal to Euodia and Syntyche. Please, because you belong to the Lord, settle your disagreement. And I ask you, my true partner, to help these two women. - Philippians 4:2-3

Euodia and Syntyche were two women in the church in Philippi who were having such a disagreement that even Paul, hundreds of miles away, had heard about it and mentioned it in his letter. Apparently their conflict was affecting the entire church. When friends get into fights, it can be painful to watch, and it usually ends up affecting many other people. You can help by praying that God will intervene. God may also want to use you to help them resolve their conflict. If so, listen to both friends with compassion. Never speak unkindly about one friend to the other, and gently help them see where they might need a change of attitude.

This Is Promising

I am praying not only for these disciples but also for all who will ever believe in Me through their message. I pray that they will all be one, just as You and I are one—as You are in Me, Father, and I am in You.
- John 17:20-21

Q

My friends are getting into some dangerous stuff and they want me to join them. How can I tell them no and still remain friends?

God's Response

[Ahab] turned to Jehoshaphat and asked, "Will you join me in battle to recover Ramoth-gilead?" Jehoshaphat replied to the king of Israel, "Why, of course! You and I are as one. My troops are your troops, and my horses are your horses.... But first let's find out what the LORD says." ... The king of Israel replied to Jehoshaphat, "There is one more man who could consult the LORD for us, but I hate him." - 1 Kings 22:4-5, 8

Ahab was a king of the north who wanted nothing to do with God. Jehoshaphat, the king of the south, was sincerely trying to follow God. Jehoshaphat made a huge mistake when he called the evil King Ahab his brother and joined him in war against the advice of God's prophet. The battle was a disaster. If your friends are pressuring you to do anything that you know would displease God, your best course of action may be to leave. Sometimes you must do more than say no; you must walk away. Otherwise, you, too, may be headed for trouble.

This Is Promising

Don't team up with those who are unbelievers. How can righteousness be a partner with wickedness? - 2 Corinthians 6:14

Q Should I tell someone about the illegal things my friends are doing? Wouldn't that mean I was betraying them?

God's Response

Do to others whatever you would like them to do to you. - Matthew 7:12

You have been called to live in freedom, my brothers and sisters. But don't use your freedom to satisfy your sinful nature. Instead, use your freedom to serve one another in love. - Galatians 5:13

There are "friends" who destroy each other, but a real friend sticks closer than a brother. - Proverbs 18:24

This is never easy. Sometimes being a true friend means doing something your friends won't understand. Which is more important to you—the safety and health of your friends, or keeping them from getting mad at you? Are your friends headed for serious trouble? Could their actions hurt someone else? If so, you must try to stop them before things get worse. Think of it this way: Would you want someone to stop you before a little problem became a huge problem that could hurt you or those around you? Being a friend sometimes means doing the hard thing for the greater good.

This Is Promising

This is My commandment: Love each other in the same way I have loved you. - John 15:12

Q My friends and I always seem to talk about other people and we usually insult them. I know that's gossip—how can I stop it?

God's Response

A troublemaker plants seeds of strife; gossip separates the best of friends.
- Proverbs 16:28

Rumors are dainty morsels that sink deep into one's heart. - Proverbs 18:8

A gossip goes around telling secrets, so don't hang around with chatterers.
- Proverbs 20:19

Fire goes out without wood, and quarrels disappear when gossip stops.
- Proverbs 26:20

It's fun to gossip, isn't it? The Bible compares rumors to "dainty morsels." Everyone loves to be in on the latest news, but the very people with whom you gossip are probably also gossiping about you. Gossip separates friends, reveals people's secrets, and causes much hurt. You can make it stop by changing the subject or by saying something kind about the person others are gossiping about. When you don't add fuel, the fire will go out.

This Is Promising
Do not spread slanderous gossip among your people. - Leviticus 19:16

Q I have a Christian friend who is starting to do bad things. How can I confront him/her?

God's Response

The LORD sent Nathan the prophet to tell David this story.... David was furious. "As surely as the LORD lives," he vowed, "any man who would do such a thing deserves to die!" ... Then Nathan said to David, "You are that man!" - 2 Samuel 12:1, 5, 7

· · · ——————— · · ·

David had done an extremely evil act (read about it in 2 Samuel 11), and God sent the prophet Nathan to confront him. Nathan helped David to see his sin by putting the situation in story form. When David realized what he had done, he repented. Sometimes a story can mirror our heart and actions. If your friend is headed the wrong direction, ask God to give you the right words that will help your friend to realize what he or she is doing. If you don't say it, who will?

This Is Promising

Wounds from a sincere friend are better than many kisses from an enemy.
- Proverbs 27:6

Q I want to be popular. Is that okay?

God's Response

Obviously, I'm not trying to win the approval of people, but of God. If pleasing people were my goal, I would not be Christ's servant.
- Galatians 1:10

Because of the miraculous signs Jesus did in Jerusalem at the Passover celebration, many began to trust in Him. But Jesus didn't trust them, because He knew human nature. No one needed to tell Him what mankind is really like. - John 2:23-25

It's not wrong to want others to like you—this is a natural human desire. The problem can come in what we are willing to do and in how we will compromise ourselves to get other people's attention. Popularity is fleeting; the person who was popular yesterday can easily be replaced by the next person who seems cooler or funnier. Jesus saw this firsthand. The crowds who adored him on Sunday called for His crucifixion less than a week later. Honor God and show love to everyone—you will be far more content, and others will admire you as well.

This Is Promising

They loved human praise more than the praise of God. - John 12:43

February

Q

I have a hard time making friends.
What should I do?

God's Response

"First let me do this one thing: Let me go up and roam in the hills and weep with my friends for two months, because I will die a virgin." ... She and her friends went into the hills and wept because she would never have children. - Judges 11:37-38

King Hiram of Tyre had always been a loyal friend of David. When Hiram learned that David's son Solomon was the new king of Israel, he sent ambassadors to congratulate him. - 1 Kings 5:1

Everyone wants to have good friends, but few are willing to invest the time and effort necessary to build such relationships. You may not make friends quickly and easily, but you can build strong, lasting friendships over time. It might help you to consider the qualities you desire in a good friend—then work to develop those qualities in your own life.

This Is Promising

Do to others whatever you would like them to do to you. - Matthew 7:12

Q I have lots of opposite-sex friends.
How can I keep those friendships pure?

God's Response

One of them was Lydia.... She was baptized along with other members of her household, and she asked us to be her guests. "If you agree that I am a true believer in the Lord," she said, "come and stay at my home." And she urged us until we agreed. - Acts 16:14-15

Paul ... said good-bye to the brothers and sisters.... Then he set sail for Syria, taking Priscilla and Aquila with him. - Acts 18:18

Opposite-sex friendships are valuable, especially since it's important that the person you marry be your friend first. As a Christian, you have a responsibility to encourage your friends to grow closer to Christ regardless of their gender. The best way to keep your friendships pure is to treat your friends like brothers and sisters. Paul gave women such as Lydia and Priscilla this kind of respect. You can do the same by training yourself to focus on your friends' heart—who they really are—rather than on just their appearance.

This Is Promising

Talk to the younger men as you would to your own brothers....
Treat younger women with all purity as you would your own sisters.
- 1 Timothy 5:1-2

If I want to be a good friend,
what are some things I should avoid?

God's Response

When three of Job's friends heard of the tragedy he had suffered, they got together and traveled from their homes to comfort and console him. Their names were Eliphaz the Temanite, Bildad the Shuhite, and Zophar the Naamathite. - Job 2:11

Job spoke again: "I have heard all this before. What miserable comforters you are! Won't you ever stop blowing hot air?" - Job 16:1-3

Job's friends were at their best when they showed up, sat with him, and listened without saying a word (see Job 2:12-13). Unfortunately, they then began to lecture Job on why they thought he was suffering and what they thought he should do about it. In the end, they even told Job that his suffering was his own fault. If only they knew the truth (read Job 1-2 for the real reason Job suffered)! A good friend is quick to listen and slow to judge. The words you speak to a friend can heal like a comforting balm or they can wound like an arrow. When your friend is hurting, the best thing you can do is to be there to listen and comfort.

This Is Promising

Never abandon a friend—either yours or your father's. When disaster strikes, you won't have to ask your brother for assistance. - Proverbs 27:10

Q How can I have a friendship with God?

God's Response

It happened just as the Scriptures say: "Abraham believed God, and God counted him as righteous because of his faith." He was even called the friend of God.- James 2:23

The LORD would speak to Moses face to face, as one speaks to a friend.... The LORD replied to Moses, "I will indeed do what you have asked, for I look favorably on you, and I know you by name." - Exodus 33:11, 17

It may seem strange to think of being friends with the God of the universe, especially since you can't see or touch Him in a physical way. It might help you to consider what makes any friendship strong: time, communication, honesty, loyalty. Friendship with God really isn't much different; it involves these same things. God has already extended an offer of friendship to you just as He did to Abraham and Moses. Like them, you can be friends with God if you truly seek Him, walk with Him, and love him.

This Is Promising

The LORD is a friend to those who fear Him. He teaches them His covenant.
- Psalm 25:14

Q How much does God love me?

God's Response

His unfailing love toward those who fear Him is as great as the height of the heavens above the earth. - Psalm 103:11

Your unfailing love is as high as the heavens. Your faithfulness reaches to the clouds. - Psalm 57:10

Long ago the LORD said to Israel: "I have loved you, My people, with an everlasting love. With unfailing love I have drawn you to Myself." - Jeremiah 31:3

· · · ———————— · · ·

It is impossible to measure God's love, which is beyond our comprehension. The Bible describes God's love for us as "unfailing," "everlasting," "as high as the heavens." God created you, loves you, and longs to have a relationship with you. So great is His love that He pursues you with persistent and unfailing love, drawing you to Himself.

This Is Promising

"The mountains may depart and the hills disappear, but even then My faithful love for you will remain. My covenant of blessing will never be broken," says the LORD, Who has mercy on you. - Isaiah 54:10

Q How can I know that God really loves me?

God's Response

The Son of Man came to seek and save those who are lost. - Luke 19:10

I am in them and You are in Me. May they experience such perfect unity that the world will know that You sent Me and that You love them as much as You love Me. - John 17:23

This hope will not lead to disappointment. For we know how dearly God loves us, because He has given us the Holy Spirit to fill our hearts with His love. - Romans 5:5

How do you know if someone really loves you? We often measure love by the price that a person is willing to pay for the one they love. God pursued you all the way to earth, became human so He could experience life as you do, and died in your place to pay for your sins. You were lost, but Jesus has found you and He won't let you go. You can find out how dearly God loves you by asking the Holy Spirit, Who lives in your heart. The Bible says that the love that fills your heart is evidence of the love God has for you.

This Is Promising
We know what real love is because Jesus gave up His life for us. - 1 John 3:16

Q How does God show His love for me?

God's Response

God loved the world so much that He gave His one and only Son,
so that everyone who believes in Him will not perish but have eternal life.
- John 3:16

There is no greater love than to lay down one's life for one's friends.
- John 15:13

See how very much our Father loves us, for He calls us His children,
and that is what we are! - 1 John 3:1

Love is usually revealed by a person's actions. If someone saved your life, wouldn't you want to know more about that person? You can know that God really loves you by learning from God's Word what He has done for you. Jesus died for you so that you can be saved from eternal death and live forever with Him. Whether or not you have accepted Him as your Lord and Savior yet, won't you get to know more about the One Who gave up so much so that you could benefit?

This Is Promising
God showed how much He loved us by sending his one and only Son into the world so that we might have eternal life through Him. - 1 John 4:9

Q How can I show God that I love Him?

God's Response

Now, Israel, what does the LORD your God require of you? He requires only that you fear the LORD your God, and live in a way that pleases Him, and love Him and serve Him with all your heart and soul. - Deuteronomy 10:12

Those who accept My commandments and obey them are the ones who love Me. - John 14:21

If you give even a cup of cold water to one of the least of My followers, you will surely be rewarded. - Matthew 10:42

We often think of "love" as a thing. We say things like "He's fallen in love," "She is lovestruck," or "They've lost their love for each other." The Bible teaches that love is really an action. Genuine love is demonstrated in conscious acts of kindness and service. You show your love for God by actively seeking a relationship with Him, by obeying Him, and by worshiping Him. You also show your love for God by serving others. Genuine love is the consistent and courageous decision to give of yourself for the well-being of others.

This Is Promising

He will not forget ... how you have shown your love to Him by caring for other believers. - Hebrews 6:10

Q

How can I serve God better?

God's Response

I will give you a new heart, and I will put a new spirit in you. I will take out your stony, stubborn heart and give you a tender, responsive heart.
- Ezekiel 36:26

You must love the LORD your God with all your heart, all your soul, and all your mind. - Matthew 22:37

· · · ———— · · ·

The kind of heart God wants you to have is a new, obedient heart that will love Him fully and really want to serve Him. You don't have to work to get that kind of heart; God will give it to you, but He won't force it on you—you have to want it. And to want it, you have to humble yourself. That means admitting that a lot of times you don't like doing things God's way. It means admitting that sometimes you're really selfish and your mind can think up some pretty bad things. Humility unlocks the door to your heart so that God can begin the clean-up process that will change you forever.

This Is Promising

Just think how much more the blood of Christ will purify our consciences from sinful deeds so that we can worship the living God. - Hebrews 9:14

Q

Is it possible to be both gentle and strong in heart?

God's Response

Never before had there been a king like Josiah, who turned to the LORD with all his heart and soul and strength. - 2 Kings 23:25

Love the LORD your God, walk in all His ways, obey His commands, hold firmly to Him, and serve Him with all your heart and all your soul. - Joshua 22:5

You will be successful if you carefully obey the decrees and regulations that the LORD gave to Israel through Moses. Be strong and courageous; do not be afraid or lose heart! - 1 Chronicles 22:13

· · · ——— · · ·

It is a myth that being gentle means being weak. On the contrary, it takes strength to humbly obey God when you are tempted to sin. It takes great courage to serve others through acts of kindness when you don't feel like it. Don't mistake power for strength. Power tries to control. Strength is the resolve not to control but to love no matter what. The biblical concept of strength is power under the control of love.

This Is Promising

Having hope will give you courage. - Job 11:18

Q Can I trust God with my whole heart?

God's Response

All heaven will praise Your great wonders, LORD; myriads of angels will praise You for Your faithfulness. - Psalm 89:5

I will be faithful to you and make you Mine, and you will finally know me as the LORD. - Hosea 2:20

He is the faithful God Who keeps His covenant for a thousand generations. - Deuteronomy 7:9

The Bible is full of stories of God's faithfulness to His people. Since the creation of the first humans, God has been faithful over and over again throughout history. If God has been faithful to so many for so long, then you can count on God to be faithful to you as well. As you watch the lives of those who have given their whole hearts to God, you will notice their complete trust in Him to guide them. This doesn't mean that their lives will be easy, but it means that they will have inner peace, joy, and confidence regardless of the circumstances. They will remember God's faithfulness in the past and know that their future is in His hands.

This Is Promising

The Lord is faithful; He will strengthen you and guard you from the evil one. - 2 Thessalonians 3:3

Q

How can I change my heart?

God's Response

Pharaoh's heart, however, remained hard. He still refused to listen, just as the LORD had predicted. - Exodus 7:13

"Oh no, sir!" [Hannah] replied, "I haven't been drinking wine or anything stronger. But I am very discouraged, and I was pouring out my heart to the LORD." - 1 Samuel 1:15

· · · ——— · · ·

Pharaoh had a hard, stubborn heart. No matter how much he heard about God or how many miracles he saw, he refused to believe. Hannah, however, continued to pray to God even when nothing seemed to happen. What is the condition of your heart? Is it hard and stubborn, or does it reach out to God whatever your circumstances? When you cut yourself off from God, you cut off your lifeline to the only One Who can really help you. A hard heart rejects the only thing that can save it—God's love. A soft heart will seek God's help and notice His perfectly timed responses.

This Is Promising

Put all your rebellion behind you, and find yourselves a new heart and a new spirit. - Ezekiel 18:31

Q I don't have a boyfriend/girlfriend and I really want one. Is that okay?

God's Response

For everything there is a season, a time for every activity under heaven.... A time to embrace and a time to turn away. - Ecclesiastes 3:1, 5

Promise me, O women of Jerusalem, by the gazelles and wild deer, not to awaken love until the time is right. - Song of Songs 2:7

· · · ———— · · ·

It's natural for you to want a relationship because God created people to need each other. The big question is how badly you want a romantic relationship. So badly that you'll take just anyone, regardless of God's standards? Good relationships with the opposite sex happen most naturally when you are not focusing on finding a boyfriend or girlfriend. A good relationship begins with a good friendship. Pursue genuine friendships, including with friends of the opposite sex, and keep serving the God Who loves you more deeply than any other friend while you wait for His perfect timing.

This Is Promising

My future is in Your hands. - Psalm 31:15

What should I look for in a potential boyfriend/girlfriend?

God's Response

Charm is deceptive, and beauty does not last; but a woman who fears the LORD will be greatly praised. - Proverbs 31:30

O LORD, God of my master, Abraham, … this is my request. I will ask one of them, "Please give me a drink from your jug." If she says, "Yes, have a drink, and I will water your camels, too!"—let her be the one you have selected as Isaac's wife. - Genesis 24:12-14

A quick coat of paint on a rusty car will help sell it, but before long the rust will creep to the surface and the new owner will realize that he's made a hasty choice that he will regret. Countless men and women have chosen a mate based solely on good looks and wound up bitterly disappointed when bad character surfaced. Train yourself to look first at the inside of a person for strong character and sincere faith in Christ. Check for the selfless qualities and actions of a real friend, for good relationships begin as good friendships. Look at the heart first, and the rest will take care of itself.

This Is Promising

The LORD said to Samuel, "Don't judge by his appearance or height.... People judge by outward appearance, but the LORD looks at the heart."
- 1 Samuel 16:7

Q Can I date someone who isn't a Christian?

God's Response

When the LORD your God brings you into the land you are about to enter and occupy, He will clear away many nations ahead of you.... Do not let your daughters and sons marry their sons and daughters, for they will lead your children away from Me to worship other gods. - Deuteronomy 7:1-4

While the verses above applied specifically to the ancient nation of Israel, they give an important principle for us to follow. Someone who is not a Christian will have different values than someone who is. If you are a Christian, God has called you to Him for a special purpose, and you have committed to living by the standards of the Bible. Going on a date with an unbeliever is one thing, but dating an unbeliever can put you in a difficult position. You might find yourself falling in love and then you just won't see things clearly. Don't put yourself in a position where you may be tempted to compromise your faith. As you look toward marriage, you need a helpmate who will encourage you to accomplish your work for God.

This Is Promising

Don't let anyone think less of you because you are young. Be an example to all believers in what you say, in the way you live, in your love, your faith, and your purity. - 1 Timothy 4:12

Q

What is okay to do physically in a dating relationship?

God's Response

Don't you realize that your body is the temple of the Holy Spirit, Who lives in you and was given to you by God? You do not belong to yourself, for God bought you with a high price. So you must honor God with your body.
- 1 Corinthians 6:19-20

Pray for us, for our conscience is clear and we want to live honorably in everything we do. - Hebrews 13:18

Physical touch between a man and a woman attracted to each other can be the spark that sets off a burning fire of emotions. We all know that a fire, if not contained, soon burns out of control, becomes increasingly difficult to stop, and can cause a great deal of damage. We don't like to admit it, but most of us know when physical touch has crossed the line and put us in danger of going too far. The Bible makes it clear that sex outside of marriage—including oral sex—is wrong. When dating, decide ahead of time what constitutes appropriate and inappropriate physical touch. Rather than trying to find out how far you can go physically, consider how you can encourage and challenge each other spiritually.

This Is Promising

A beautiful woman who lacks discretion is like a gold ring in a pig's snout.
- Proverbs 11:22

All of my friends think that sex before marriage is okay—in fact, it's sort of expected. What does the Bible say about premarital sex?

God's Response

Potiphar's wife soon began to look at him lustfully. "Come and sleep with me," she demanded. But Joseph refused.... "How could I do such a wicked thing? It would be a great sin against God." ... She came and grabbed him by his cloak, demanding, "Come on, sleep with me!" Joseph tore himself away. - Genesis 39:7-9, 12

Joseph drew his boundaries early, knowing that sex outside of marriage is "a great sin against God." When temptation came, he was prepared and he knew how to handle it. Even though everyone around you seems to assume that premarital sex is okay, they do not see the whole picture: unwanted pregnancy, disease, guilt, shame, and secrets kept from your future spouse. The Bible sets boundaries—not to curb your fun, but to protect you and show you how to have the greatest joy and fulfillment in a relationship. It's interesting that virtually all sex surveys show greater sexual satisfaction among married couples than unmarried couples. God knows what He's doing when He asks us to reserve sex for marriage.

This Is Promising

God's will is for you to be holy, so stay away from all sexual sin. Then each of you will control his own body and live in holiness and honor—not in lustful passion. - 1 Thessalonians 4:3-5

Q What does God think about sex?

God's Response

This explains why a man leaves his father and mother and is joined to his wife, and the two are united into one. - Genesis 2:24

Because there is so much sexual immorality, each man should have his own wife, and each woman should have her own husband. The husband should fulfill his wife's sexual needs, and the wife should fulfill her husband's needs. - 1 Corinthians 7:2-3

Here is a strange thought—God likes sex! God created sex, making men and women as sexual beings to reproduce and replenish the next generation and as a means to express love and delight in one another. Think of it: He could have created us to reproduce by spores that float through the air; instead, He made sex a source of great enjoyment. God created sex for emotional and physical oneness between a married man and woman. This is also a picture of the loyalty and intimacy a believer can have with God. Those who enjoy sex within the boundaries created by God will find the most fulfillment in their marriage.

This Is Promising

You can't say that our bodies were made for sexual immorality. They were made for the Lord, and the Lord cares about our bodies. - 1 Corinthians 6:13

Q

What is wrong with just thinking about having sex with someone?

God's Response

I say, anyone who even looks at a woman with lust has already committed adultery with her in his heart. - Matthew 5:28

It is what comes from inside that defiles you. For from within, out of a person's heart, come evil thoughts, sexual immorality … lustful desires. - Mark 7:20-22

... ——— ...

What you think about doesn't just come from your mind; it comes from your heart. Your thoughts tell you the condition of your heart because your every action begins as a thought. Left unchecked, wrong thoughts will eventually result in wrong actions. If you continue to think about having sex with someone, your heart will begin to convince your mind that what you want to do is okay. The Bible says that the heart is "desperately wicked" (Jeremiah 17:9). In other words, don't trust your emotions to tell you what is right and good. Trust God's Word, for it comes from God's heart, which is good and perfect.

This Is Promising

Guard your heart above all else, for it determines the course of your life.
- Proverbs 4:23

Q Why is virginity so important?
How can I maintain my virginity?

God's Response

All who have this eager expectation will keep themselves pure, just as He is pure. - 1 John 3:3

If you keep yourself pure, you will be a special utensil for honorable use. Your life will be clean, and you will be ready for the Master to use you for every good work. - 2 Timothy 2:21

God gave you the gift of your virginity and He allows you to choose whom you will give it to. You can give it to only one person in the whole world. Don't give this precious gift away to just anyone, but save it for the person who commits to you by marrying you. This is why God commands you not to have sex before marriage—He is trying to protect you from people who will hurt you by stealing your purity without committing to you.

This Is Promising

Give honor to marriage, and remain faithful to one another in marriage. God will surely judge people who are immoral and those who commit adultery. - Hebrews 13:4

Q Will God forgive my past sexual sins?
Can I truly start over?

God's Response

Joshua secretly sent out two spies from the Israelite camp at Acacia....
So the two men set out and came to the house of a prostitute named
Rahab and stayed there that night.... Rahab went up on the roof to talk
with them. "I know the LORD has given you this land," she told them.
- Joshua 2:1, 8-9

It was by faith that Rahab the prostitute was not destroyed with the people
in her city who refused to obey God. - Hebrews 11:31

· · · ———————— · · ·

It is difficult to believe that God could completely forgive us, especially when we have such a difficult time forgiving ourselves. The beauty of the Christian faith is that we have a God Who will wipe the slate clean and give us a fresh start no matter how much we've sinned. You need to confess your sin, draw the boundary lines, and decide you will not cross them again until you are married. Rahab was a prostitute who, through faith in God, was saved when Jericho fell. Her name later appears in the genealogy of Jesus (Matthew 1:5). God hasn't given up on you, so don't give up on yourself. When you are forgiven, God looks at you as though you had never sinned.

This Is Promising

Oh, what joy for those whose disobedience is forgiven, whose sin is put out
of sight! - Psalm 32:1

Q How will I know when I've met the person I should marry?

God's Response

His father and mother objected. "Isn't there even one woman in our tribe or among all the Israelites you could marry?" they asked. "Why must you go to the pagan Philistines to find a wife?" But Samson told his father, "Get her for me! She looks good to me." - Judges 14:3

Some time later Samson fell in love with a woman named Delilah, who lived in the valley of Sorek. The rulers of the Philistines went to her and said, "Entice Samson to tell you what makes him so strong." - Judges 16:4-5

Samson never did get a clue. He wanted what looked good to him, regardless of the girl's character or the advice of his parents. As you date people, look for godly character in them. Ask God right from the start to show you who would be a good mate for you. As you focus more on someone's character and integrity and less on outward appearance, your discernment will grow. Does God have a specific person for you to marry? The Bible isn't clear about that, but it is absolutely clear on the kind of person you should marry. The closer you get to God, the clearer that choice will be.

This Is Promising

He will guide us until we die. - Psalm 48:14

Q Is there really somebody for everyone?
Should everyone get married?

God's Response

God gives to some the gift of marriage, and to others the gift of singleness.
- 1 Corinthians 7:7

Marriage is not for everyone. Both marriage and singleness are gifts from God. If you are married, consider your spouse a gift from God and honor God and your spouse with your marriage. If you remain single or become single again after marrying, honor God in your singleness and look for ways to be a blessing to others. Paul, who was single, wished that more people could devote themselves so completely to the ministry of God's Word. If you are single, don't spend your time pining away for marriage. Instead, draw closer to God, seek to grow more mature in your faith, and serve wherever God calls you.

This Is Promising

Each of you should continue to live in whatever situation the Lord has placed you. - 1 Corinthians 7:17

Q My friend's parents are getting a divorce.
It seems like everyone gets divorced.
Should I just expect that for myself?

God's Response

You cry out, "Why doesn't the LORD accept my worship?" I'll tell you why! Because the LORD witnessed the vows you and your wife made when you were young.... "For I hate divorce!" says the LORD, the God of Israel.... "So guard your heart; do not be unfaithful to your wife." - Malachi 2:14-16

Many things that are common in our society are contrary to God's design and desire for us. As a Christian, you should not regard divorce as an option. If you go into marriage committed to finding a way through your problems rather than a way out, your chances of divorce will be less. Then, when the first major conflict arises, your first instinct will be to resolve the conflict, not dissolve the marriage. Work through every difficulty with God's help, which may include the help of a godly Christian counselor. You don't need to be a statistic. The vows you say on your wedding day are symbolic of the vows of commitment you have made to honor God for your whole life.

This Is Promising

Since they are no longer two but one, let no one split apart what God has joined together. - Matthew 19:6

Q

I've been hurt deeply.
How do I recover from a broken heart?

God's Response

Their insults have broken my heart, and I am in despair. If only one person would show some pity; if only one would turn and comfort me.... For the LORD hears the cries of the needy; He does not despise His imprisoned people. - Psalm 69:20, 33

He heals the brokenhearted and bandages their wounds. - Psalm 147:3

God has experienced brokenness and He understands it. No matter how strong you think you must be, a broken heart still hurts to the core. Whether you were hurt by a parent, a friend, a boyfriend, or a girlfriend, God grieves with you when you hurt and He is ready to provide comfort. A broken heart often takes a while to heal. It is comforting to know that even though we have broken God's heart repeatedly, He still loves us and wants to comfort us in our brokenness.

This Is Promising

Whatever happens, my dear brothers and sisters, rejoice in the Lord.
- Philippians 3:1

Q The Bible talks about intimacy with God. What does that mean?

God's Response

"When that day comes," says the LORD, "you will call Me 'my husband' instead of 'my master.' … I will make you My wife forever, showing you righteousness and justice, unfailing love and compassion." - Hosea 2:16, 19

See how very much our Father loves us, for He calls us His children.
- 1 John 3:1

· · · ——— · · ·

There is no image that can completely express the kind of relationship God wants to have with you. The Bible uses images of the love between husband and wife or father and child to give us some glimpse of it. God already knows your heart, your thoughts, your motives, your dreams, and He wants to make you the best you can be. When you accept that and draw nearer to Him, you will begin to know Him intimately, and you will experience a love relationship that nothing else can compare to.

This Is Promising

Those who wish to boast should boast in this alone: that they truly know Me and understand that I am the LORD Who demonstrates unfailing love and Who brings justice and righteousness to the earth, and that I delight in these things. I, the LORD, have spoken! - Jeremiah 9:24

Q

What must I do to experience intimacy with God?

God's Response

My heart has heard You say, "Come and talk with Me." And my heart responds, "LORD, I am coming." - Psalm 27:8

The LORD is close to all who call on Him, yes, to all who call on Him in truth. - Psalm 145:18

Come close to God, and God will come close to you. - James 4:8

When you have a close friend, you do your best to stay in touch with him or her. It's no different with God. He promises that as you draw close to Him, He will draw close to you. How do you draw close to Him? Read His Word daily and listen to what He says to you through it. Pray constantly. Remember that God is with you all day, every day, and talk to Him about everything that comes up at school, at home, at work, and on the practice field. Share your thoughts, needs, and concerns with Him. As you practice remembering His presence, you'll begin to gain the intimacy you desire.

This Is Promising

If you seek Him, you will find Him. - 1 Chronicles 28:9

Q

Why does the Bible tell me to guard my heart? How do I do that?

God's Response

Guard your heart above all else, for it determines the course of your life.
- Proverbs 4:23

Dear children, keep away from anything that might take God's place in your hearts. - 1 John 5:21

My child, listen and be wise: Keep your heart on the right course.
- Proverbs 23:19

The purpose of a guardrail on a dangerous curve is not to inhibit your freedom to drive, but to save your life! That guardrail is a sign of security and safety, not an obstacle to flying. In the same way, you need a guardrail as you travel through life—not to inhibit your freedom, but to keep your life from going out of control. Your heart determines where you go because it most affects your passions. If you don't guard your heart with God's Word and stay focused on the road God has put you on, you may have a terrible accident when temptation distracts you.

This Is Promising

These were his instructions to them: "You must always act in the fear of the LORD, with faithfulness and an undivided heart." - 2 Chronicles 19:9

March

Q If God really loves me,
why is my life so difficult?

God's Response

Then Goliath, a Philistine champion from Gath, came out of the Philistine ranks to face the forces of Israel. He was over nine feet tall! ... David asked the soldiers standing nearby, ... "Who is this pagan Philistine anyway, that he is allowed to defy the armies of the living God?" ... [David] picked up five smooth stones from a stream and put them into his shepherd's bag. Then, armed only with his shepherd's staff and sling, he started across the valley to fight the Philistine. - 1 Samuel 17:4, 26, 40

Your life may be filled with giant problems—relationship problems, financial difficulties, or physical limitations. The presence of problems doesn't mean that God is absent or that He doesn't love you. Problems come to everyone, but with God, you have the resources to deal with any giant problem that comes your way.

This Is Promising

Here on earth you will have many trials and sorrows. But take heart, because I have overcome the world. - John 16:33

Q If God really loves me, why doesn't he answer my prayers?

God's Response

The two sisters sent a message to Jesus telling him, "Lord, your dear friend is very sick." But when Jesus heard about it He said, "Lazarus's sickness will not end in death. No, it happened for the glory of God so that the Son of God will receive glory from this." So although Jesus loved Martha, Mary, and Lazarus, He stayed where He was for the next two days. - John 11:3-6

What do you do when God seems to be silent? When you think that God is refusing to answer, He may be telling you "no"—and you don't want to hear it—or He may simply be waiting for his perfect timing to send you His answer. Mary and Martha didn't understand why Jesus didn't answer their prayer to come and heal their brother. Jesus waited because He had an answer better than anything they could imagine. God's answer will come—and it may be better than your best dreams.

This Is Promising

He does not ignore the cries of those who suffer. - Psalm 9:12

Q If God really loves me,
why do I feel so uncertain?

God's Response

*As Pharaoh approached, the people of Israel looked up and panicked
when they saw the Egyptians overtaking them. They cried out to the
LORD, and they said to Moses, "Why did you bring us out here to die in
the wilderness? … Didn't we tell you this would happen while we were
still in Egypt? We said, 'Leave us alone! Let us be slaves to the Egyptians.
It's better to be a slave in Egypt than a corpse in the wilderness!' "*
- Exodus 14:10-12

Faith is the confidence that what we hope for will actually happen.
- Hebrews 11:1

If you had asked the Israelites at that moment if God loved them,
they would have responded that it certainly didn't feel like it—not
with all that was going wrong for them just then. Moses knew
enough to trust God and His promises. Don't depend on your
feelings or your circumstances to feel loved. Instead, remember all
that God has done to show His love for you, and trust that He knows
what is best for you. Feelings will come and go, but God is faithful!

This Is Promising

*Moses told the people, "Don't be afraid. Just stand still and watch the LORD
rescue you today." - Exodus 14:13*

Q If God really loves me, why do I feel like a nobody in the crowds at school?

God's Response

O LORD, … You know everything I do…. Such knowledge is too wonderful for me. - Psalm 139:1-3, 6

The very hairs on your head are all numbered. So don't be afraid; you are more valuable to God than a whole flock of sparrows. - Luke 12:7

There are different kinds of spiritual gifts, but the same Spirit is the source of them all…. A spiritual gift is given to each of us so we can help each other. - 1 Corinthians 12:4, 7

You may feel that you disappear into the crowd, but you are not invisible to God, Who knows everything about you. He created you for a relationship with Him and gave you a purpose in life. No one else is like you or can do what He created you to do, so He gave you a special role on earth. This makes you extremely valuable to Him. As you walk through the crowds today, remember that you are somebody special to God. Get close to Him so that you can feel His love and discover what He wants you to do.

This Is Promising

I am with you always, even to the end of the age. - Matthew 28:20

Q Am I really important to God?

God's Response

You have not received a spirit that makes you fearful slaves. Instead, you received God's Spirit when He adopted you as His own children. Now we call Him, "Abba, Father." For His Spirit joins with our spirit to affirm that we are God's children. And since we are His children, we are His heirs. In fact, together with Christ we are heirs of God's glory. - Romans 8:15-17

Adopted children sometimes struggle with the love of their birth parents and their adoptive parents, but every orphan longs to be adopted into a loving family. God has chosen you and adopted you into His family; He loves you as His precious child. He has even given you an inheritance as His very own! You can't get more important than that!

This Is Promising

To all who believed Him and accepted Him, He gave the right to become children of God. - John 1:12

Q What am I worth? What is my value to God?

God's Response

When I look at the night sky and see the work of Your fingers … what are people that You should think about them, mere mortals that You should care for them? … You gave them charge of everything You made.
- Psalm 8:3-6

God showed how much He loved us by sending His one and only Son into the world so that we might have eternal life through Him. This is real love—not that we loved God, but that He loved us and sent His Son as a sacrifice to take away our sins. - 1 John 4:9-10

What makes something valuable? One way to determine value is to consider the price that was paid for it. Another measure of value is the uniqueness and purpose of the object. When God created you, He uniquely designed you for His purpose because He loves you and has a plan for you. God has paid the ultimate price for you in sending His Son to die for you! You are of immeasurable value to God. You are priceless.

This Is Promising
God loved the world so much that He gave His one and only Son, so that everyone who believes in Him will not perish but have eternal life.
- John 3:16

When Bad Things Happen

Q If God really loves people, why do such bad things happen in the world?

God's Response

I have called you by name; you are Mine. When you go through deep waters, I will be with you. When you go through rivers of difficulty, you will not drown. When you walk through the fire of oppression, you will not be burned up; the flames will not consume you. - Isaiah 43:1-2

The world is full of suffering—you see it every time you turn on the TV. If God is so loving and so powerful, why do these things happen? Why doesn't He stop them? The answer is that He will. God promises a world like that—we call it heaven, but the Bible calls it the new earth, restored to be the way that God originally created it. In the meantime, we must deal with the evil that exists, trusting that God is able to bring good out of the bad things in the world.

This Is Promising

I heard a loud shout from the throne, saying, "Look, God's home is now among His people! He will live with them, and they will be His people. God Himself will be with them. He will wipe every tear from their eyes, and there will be no more death or sorrow or crying or pain. All these things are gone forever." - Revelation 21:3-4

Q What does it mean to trust God?

God's Response

This was [the spies'] report to Moses: "We entered the land you sent us to explore, and it is indeed a bountiful country.... But the people living there are powerful, and their towns are large and fortified." ... But Caleb tried to quiet the people as they stood before Moses. "Let's go at once to take the land," he said. "We can certainly conquer it!" - Numbers 13:27-30

The size of the warriors and their cities paralyzed God's people, but Caleb trusted God. Sure, he had seen the fortified cities and noticed the giant people, but he remembered God's promise that the land was theirs. If you know that God is leading you to a certain place, don't let the size of the obstacles paralyze you. Carefully evaluate what's before you, as Caleb did. Then, if you still feel God's confirmation, move ahead, and watch the obstacles fall as God clears the way for you.

This Is Promising

My servant Caleb has a different attitude than the others have. He has remained loyal to Me, so I will bring him into the land he explored.
- Numbers 14:24

Q

What makes God trustworthy?

God's Response

Not one of you from this wicked generation will live to see the good land I swore to give your ancestors, except Caleb son of Jephunneh. He will see this land because he has followed the LORD completely. I will give to him and his descendants some of the very land he explored during his scouting mission. - Deuteronomy 1:35-36

Joshua blessed Caleb son of Jephunneh and gave Hebron to him as his portion of land … because he wholeheartedly followed the LORD, the God of Israel. - Joshua 14:13-14

God is trustworthy because He keeps His promises. Caleb trusted in God even when the rest of the Israelites rebelled. Caleb had to wander with the nation for those forty years of punishment, but while the others were dying off, Caleb was kept alive. When the nation finally entered the land, Caleb received his reward—and he was still strong enough to fight for it! Like Caleb, trust God to keep His promises. The Bible is full of promises that relate directly to you.

This Is Promising

Those who know Your name trust in You, for You, O LORD, do not abandon those who search for You. - Psalm 9:10

Q

How can I avoid trusting the wrong people or the wrong things?

God's Response

Without consulting Me, you have gone down to Egypt for help. You have put your trust in Pharaoh's protection. You have tried to hide in his shade. But by trusting Pharaoh, you will be humiliated, and by depending on him, you will be disgraced. - Isaiah 30:2-3

Putting confidence in an unreliable person in times of trouble is like chewing with a broken tooth or walking on a lame foot. - Proverbs 25:19

Trust is a tricky thing. Knowing whom you can trust is not always clear, especially when you look around and see so many people in high positions who abuse their power and hurt those who depend on them. What can you do? Begin by observing the character and actions of people around you. Notice who is consistently truthful and reliable. Who treats others as they would like to be treated? Keep in mind that even the most godly person will make mistakes and sometimes let you down, so don't look to people to give you what only God can provide. Only God is completely trustworthy.

This Is Promising

It is better to take refuge in the LORD than to trust in people. It is better to take refuge in the LORD than to trust in princes. - Psalm 118:8-9

Q How do I know God will keep His promises?

God's Response

God has given us both His promise and His oath. These two things are unchangeable because it is impossible for God to lie. - Hebrews 6:18

No, I will not break My covenant; I will not take back a single word I said.... I cannot lie. - Psalm 89:34-35

This truth gives them confidence that they have eternal life, which God— Who does not lie—promised them before the world began. - Titus 1:2

Have you ever wondered if there is anything that God cannot do? Well, actually there is something God can't do. He cannot lie. He is truth, and the source of all truth. God's promises are completely dependable and trustworthy because God cannot go back on His word. This can give you great comfort, today and in the future. It is amazing to discover how many promises God has made in the Bible to everyone who trusts Him. Find those promises, believe them, and see how trustworthy God is.

This Is Promising

Let us hold tightly without wavering to the hope we affirm, for God can be trusted to keep His promise. - Hebrews 10:23

Q

What promises has God made that matter to me in my life today?

God's Response

The LORD your God will personally go ahead of you. He will neither fail you nor abandon you. - Deuteronomy 31:6

If we confess our sins to Him, He is faithful and just to forgive us our sins and to cleanse us from all wickedness. - 1 John 1:9

We have peace with God because of what Jesus Christ our Lord has done for us. - Romans 5:1

Come to Me, all of you who are weary and carry heavy burdens, and I will give you rest…. You will find rest for your souls. - Matthew 11:28-29

Sometimes God seems distant and even irrelevant to our daily lives. Consider the promises in the above verses. God has promised to forgive your sins, to give you peace of heart and mind, to carry your burdens, and to give you rest. How much more meaningful and relevant to your life could His promises be? Which of these promises do you most need to hold on to today? Thank God that He has promised all of this and that He is faithful.

This Is Promising

He prayed, "O LORD, God of Israel, there is no God like You in all of heaven above or on the earth below. You keep Your covenant and show unfailing love to all who walk before You in wholehearted devotion." - 1 Kings 8:23

Q

What should I do when I feel discouraged?

God's Response

Listen, all you people of Judah and Jerusalem! Listen, King Jehoshaphat! This is what the LORD says: Do not be afraid! Don't be discouraged by this mighty army, for the battle is not yours, but God's.... You will not even need to fight. Take your positions; then stand still and watch the LORD's victory. He is with you, O people of Judah and Jerusalem. Do not be afraid or discouraged. Go out against them tomorrow, for the LORD is with you!
- 2 Chronicles 20:15-17

Do you ever feel that life is a battle and that you are on the losing side? Life can be very discouraging. When you are tired or when the obstacles seem too big, it is easy to feel down. Remember that when you have God's Spirit in you, you are tapped into God's almighty power. You don't have to win every battle on your own—God doesn't even want you to. When you ask for His help in your struggles, God will fight for you.

This Is Promising

Do not be afraid or discouraged. For the LORD your God is with you wherever you go. - Joshua 1:9

Q Does God care when I feel depressed?

God's Response

From the depths of despair, O LORD, I call for Your help. - Psalm 130:1

Come quickly, LORD, and answer me, for my depression deepens. Don't turn away from me, or I will die. - Psalm 143:7

God blesses those who mourn, for they will be comforted. - Matthew 5:4

[Jesus] told them, "My soul is crushed with grief to the point of death." - Matthew 26:38

Depression can be serious, often requiring counseling and even medical attention. It also requires spiritual attention. Jesus understands what it feels like to have your soul crushed to the point of death and to live through what some call "the dark night of the soul." When you feel this low, you may feel hopeless. However, the darkness of depression doesn't have to block out the light of God's healing. Cry out to Him even from your darkness. He will hear and comfort you, hold you, and begin to heal you.

This Is Promising

Even in darkness I cannot hide from You. To You the night shines as bright as day. Darkness and light are the same to You. - Psalm 139:12

What can I do when I'm depressed?
How can I recover?

God's Response

Great is the LORD! He is most worthy of praise! He is to be feared above all gods. - 1 Chronicles 16:25

He comforts us in all our troubles so that we can comfort others. When they are troubled, we will be able to give them the same comfort God has given us. - 2 Corinthians 1:4

Depression often involves a kind of self-obsession in which all you are able to see is your own problems, pain, and despair. When you withdraw into yourself this way, it becomes almost impossible to see things clearly. One way to deal with this is to start praising God for everything you can think of: His greatness, His love, all He has done for you, and how valuable you are to Him. It may be helpful for you to offer help and comfort to others in need. Praising God will draw your focus away from yourself, and helping others will put your problems in perspective.

This Is Promising

May Your gracious Spirit lead me forward on a firm footing. - Psalm 143:10

Q Are feelings of depression sinful?

God's Response

"O God my rock," I cry, "Why have You forgotten me? Why must I wander around in grief, oppressed by my enemies?" Their taunts break my bones. They scoff, "Where is this God of yours?" Why am I discouraged? Why is my heart so sad? I will put my hope in God! I will praise Him again—my Savior and my God! - Psalm 42:9-11

You can't feel much lower than David did when he wrote this psalm. These kinds of feelings are not necessarily sinful, but your actions and thoughts can be if you allow your feelings to overwhelm you. Your feelings of depression may tempt you to turn away from God and others. Tell God how you are feeling. Don't be afraid to be brutally honest with Him, as David was. He can handle it and He can help you.

This Is Promising

I waited patiently for the LORD to help me, and He turned to me and heard my cry. He lifted me out of the pit of despair, out of the mud and the mire. He set my feet on solid ground and steadied me as I walked along.
- Psalm 40:1-2

Q

Does feeling depressed mean
that my faith isn't real?

God's Response

*Jezebel sent this message to Elijah: "May the gods strike me and even kill
me if by this time tomorrow I have not killed you just as you killed them."
Elijah was afraid and fled for his life.... He sat down under a solitary
broom tree and prayed that he might die. "I have had enough, LORD," he
said. "Take my life, for I am no better than my ancestors." - 1 Kings 19:2-4*

Have you ever noticed that the lows of depression often come after
great spiritual highs? Having real faith doesn't mean that you never
experience low periods. Elijah had just experienced a great victory
for God (see 1 Kings 18); here, he prays to die. His faith was very
real, but he was exhausted and afraid. God let him sleep and fed
him before sending him back to work. If you're feeling depressed,
take care of your physical needs for rest and nourishment and hold
on to God through the darkness.

This Is Promising

*From the depths of despair, O LORD, I call for Your help.... I am counting on
the LORD; yes, I am counting on Him. I have put my hope in His word.*
- Psalm 130:1, 5

Q

How can I help a friend who seems discouraged or depressed?

God's Response

Be happy with those who are happy, and weep with those who weep.
- Romans 12:15

Singing cheerful songs to a person with a heavy heart is like taking someone's coat in cold weather or pouring vinegar in a wound.
- Proverbs 25:20

I was glad when they said to me, "Let us go to the house of the LORD."
- Psalm 122:1

Two things are often helpful—modeling the gentle, caring love of Christ, and helping your friend through the darkness by keeping him or her involved with other Christians. Depressed people often pull away and withdraw from others. Those dealing with depression need comfort and understanding, not advice and lectures. You can help a depressed person by your quiet presence, your love, and your encouragement.

This Is Promising

When he saw the strong wind and the waves, he was terrified and began to sink. "Save me, Lord!" he shouted. Jesus immediately reached out and grabbed him. - Matthew 14:30-31

Q

Some days I feel great; other days I feel terrible. Is that normal? What should I do?

God's Response

Always be full of joy in the Lord. I say it again—rejoice! Let everyone see that you are considerate in all you do. - Philippians 4:4-5

I have learned how to be content with whatever I have. I know how to live on almost nothing or with everything. I have learned the secret of living in every situation, whether it is with a full stomach or empty, with plenty or little. - Philippians 4:11-12

· · · ———————— · · ·

We are emotional beings because God created us with feelings. It is not unusual or abnormal to experience emotional and spiritual highs and lows in short periods of time. However, the joy and contentment to which these verses refer run much deeper than the emotions of the moment. This kind of joy is like a strong current that runs deep beneath the stormy surface of your feelings.

This Is Promising

The Holy Spirit produces this kind of fruit in our lives: … joy. - Galatians 5:22

Q How can I keep my anger from controlling my actions?

God's Response

"Don't sin by letting anger control you." Don't let the sun go down while you are still angry, for anger gives a foothold to the devil.
- Ephesians 4:26-27

Get rid of all bitterness, rage, anger, harsh words, and slander, as well as all types of evil behavior. Instead, be kind to each other, tenderhearted, forgiving one another, just as God through Christ has forgiven you.
- Ephesians 4:31-32

Anger is not necessarily sinful, but it easily becomes a breeding ground for sinful thoughts and actions if it is not dealt with. Determine not to let your anger fester. Find ways to resolve conflict as quickly as possible so that your anger doesn't give the devil a foothold. Bitterness and resentment are poisons that will consume you unless you can find a way to forgive and leave your pain in God's hands. His Holy Spirit has the power to help you do this if you ask.

This Is Promising

The Holy Spirit produces this kind of fruit in our lives: ... self-control.
- Galatians 5:22-23

Q How can I be sure that I'm saved?

God's Response

God loved the world so much that He gave His one and only Son, so that everyone who believes in Him will not perish but have eternal life.
- John 3:16

Now he has made all of this plain to us by the appearing of Christ Jesus, our Savior. He broke the power of death and illuminated the way to life and immortality through the Good News.... I know the One in whom I trust, and I am sure that He is able to guard what I have entrusted to Him until the day of His return. - 2 Timothy 1:10-12

· · · ———— · · ·

The simple and easy answer is "because the Bible says so." That sounds ridiculously trite, but it really is true. Assurance does not come from how good or faithful you are, but from how good and faithful God is. Assurance does not come from your feelings; it comes from the Word of God. When this truth begins to sink into your soul, then you will have the growing confidence that if you have accepted Jesus Christ as Savior, His promise of salvation applies to you.

This Is Promising

If you confess with your mouth that Jesus is Lord and believe in your heart that God raised Him from the dead, you will be saved. - Romans 10:9

Q

Does being a Christian make a difference in my everyday life?

God's Response

We are no longer slaves to sin. For when we died with Christ we were set free from the power of sin. And since we died with Christ, we know we will also live with Him. - Romans 6:6-8

He has created us anew in Christ Jesus, so we can do the good things He planned for us long ago. - Ephesians 2:10

What is freedom? Many people today would define it as the ability to do whatever they want whenever they want. Ironically, the Bible says that those who reject God have less freedom because they are slaves to sin. The biblical understanding of freedom is living the way you were created to live. When you become a Christian you will still sin, but you will no longer be enslaved to sin. You are free to live as God created you to live—assured that your life has purpose, free to use your talents and abilities, full of hope for the future, and confident of God's love.

This Is Promising

Anyone who belongs to Christ has become a new person. The old life is gone; a new life has begun! - 2 Corinthians 5:17

Q How can I be sure that I will have eternal life?

God's Response

Soon the world will no longer see Me, but you will see Me. Since I live, you also will live. - John 14:19

Jesus told her, "I am the resurrection and the life. Anyone who believes in Me will live, even after dying. Everyone who lives in Me and believes in Me will never ever die." - John 11:25-26

In fact, Christ has been raised from the dead. He is the first of a great harvest of all who have died. - 1 Corinthians 15:20

. . . ——— . . .

This is a tough question. First consider this question: Can you believe that Jesus was God's Son, that He lived a perfect life on earth, died on the cross to pay for your sins, and rose from the dead? If you can believe all this about Jesus, then you have no reason to doubt His promises to you. He promised eternal life to all believers, and He proved it by his ability to overcome death.

This Is Promising

I have written this to you who believe in the name of the Son of God, so that you may know you have eternal life. - 1 John 5:13

Q Can anyone become a Christian?

God's Response

"The message is very close at hand; it is on your lips and in your heart."
And that message is the very message about faith that we preach: If you
confess with your mouth that Jesus is Lord and believe in your heart that
God raised Him from the dead, you will be saved. For it is by believing in
your heart that you are made right with God, and it is by confessing with
your mouth that you are saved.... For "Everyone who calls on the name of
the LORD will be saved." - Romans 10:8-10, 13

Salvation may be an obscure religious word, but for the Christian,
it is actually a very simple concept. People think that it must be a
complicated process, but it is not. Salvation is available to anyone,
regardless of social standing, race, financial status, past problems,
or fears. When people believe in their hearts and say with their
mouths that Christ is the risen Lord, they will be saved. Just be
sincere—all He wants is your heart.

This Is Promising
The Lord ... does not want anyone to be destroyed, but wants everyone to
repent. - 2 Peter 3:9

Q Why did Jesus have to die on the cross in order to save us?

God's Response

Now He has reconciled you to Himself through the death of Christ in His physical body. As a result, He has brought you into His own presence, and you are holy and blameless as you stand before Him without a single fault.
- Colossians 1:22

The wages of sin is death, but the free gift of God is eternal life through Christ Jesus our Lord. - Romans 6:23

The cross can be either a barrier or a bridge to God. The Bible calls it a stumbling block and foolishness to those who don't "get it" (1 Corinthians 1:23). The Bible says that every person since the beginning of time has sinned, and that sin is rebellion against God. God is holy—perfect—and cannot live eternally alongside sin. That's not His idea of a perfect world. Sin has to go if you want to live with God forever, so either you separate yourself and your sin from God, or God takes your sin away so you can be perfect in His eyes. God chose to have His Son, Jesus, take your punishment so you wouldn't have to. Accept His gift of taking away your punishment so you can live forever with Him. This is the greatest gift ever offered—don't refuse it!

This Is Promising

Christ died for us so that, whether we are dead or alive when He returns, we can live with Him forever. - 1 Thessalonians 5:10

Q   What does Jesus' death mean for me?

God's Response

He personally carried our sins in His body on the cross so that we can be dead to sin and live for what is right. By His wounds you are healed.
- 1 Peter 2:24

He canceled the record of the charges against us and took it away by nailing it to the cross. - Colossians 2:14

If there were no consequences for driving through red lights, breaking into people's homes, or killing people, anarchy would reign. The things people value most—peace, order, security—would be gone. Sin is breaking the laws that the Creator of the universe set up to bring peace, order, and security to our world. Breaking God's laws brings God's punishment just as breaking government laws brings civil punishment. The good news is this: When Jesus died on the cross, He took the punishment for sin that we deserve. Sin no longer controls us now, and one day we will be rid of sin forever.

This Is Promising

God in all His fullness was pleased to live in Christ, and through Him God reconciled everything to Himself. He made peace with everything in heaven and on earth by means of Christ's blood on the cross. This includes you who were once far away from God. - Colossians 1:19-21

Q

What does Jesus' resurrection mean for me?

God's Response

Jesus looked up to heaven and said, "Father, thank You for hearing Me. You always hear Me, but I said it out loud for the sake of all these people standing here, so that they will believe You sent Me." Then Jesus shouted, "Lazarus, come out!" And the dead man came out, his hands and feet bound in graveclothes, his face wrapped in a headcloth. Jesus told them, "Unwrap him and let him go!" - John 11:41-44

Jesus showed that He had power over death by raising Lazarus. One day Lazarus would die again, but he could also be assured of being raised again—not to life on earth, but to eternity in heaven. Because Jesus rose from the dead with a new body, you can be assured of His power over death. This same power defeats Satan and guarantees that if you believe in Jesus you, too, will be resurrected one day with a new body and live forever in heaven. For Christians, the Resurrection is everything!

This Is Promising

If Christ has not been raised, then your faith is useless and you are still guilty of your sins. - 1 Corinthians 15:17

Q What is eternal life going to be like?

God's Response

Look, God's home is now among His people! He will live with them, and they will be His people. God Himself will be with them. He will wipe every tear from their eyes, and there will be no more death or sorrow or crying or pain. All these things are gone forever. - Revelation 21:3-4

- - - · · · - - -

Eternity is not an extension of life here on earth, where you suffer, grieve, and feel hurt. Instead, God promises something new. He will restore this earth to be the way He once created it—as a beautiful place with no sin, sorrow, or pain. You will live in the world you long for that is without evil and suffering. God created humans for this earth, so the new earth will have a lot of similarities to this one, but it will be better and more amazing in every way. You will be in God's presence, forever filled with joy. You don't have to worry about strumming a harp on some cloud. There will be plenty to do that will be fun, fulfilling, and purposeful.

This Is Promising

No eye has seen, no ear has heard, and no mind has imagined what God has prepared for those who love Him. - 1 Corinthians 2:9

Q What will my body be like after it is resurrected?

God's Response

Our bodies are buried in brokenness, but they will be raised in glory.
They are buried in weakness, but they will be raised in strength. They are
buried as natural human bodies, but they will be raised as spiritual bodies.
For just as there are natural bodies, there are also spiritual bodies....
Our physical bodies cannot inherit the Kingdom of God. These dying
bodies cannot inherit what will last forever. - 1 Corinthians 15:43-44, 50

Your resurrected body will be a literal, physical body like the one
you have now, and it will also have many supernatural characteristics. You may be able to walk through walls as Jesus did with
His resurrected body. More importantly, your new body won't ever
decay from the effects of sin. You will never be sick or in pain again,
nor will your mind think sinful thoughts. You will never again
compare yourself to other bodies or wish that you were different.
You will be fully and finally perfect in God's sight.

This Is Promising

Our earthly bodies are planted in the ground when we die, but they will be
raised to live forever. - 1 Corinthians 15:42

Q Who is the Holy Spirit?

God's Response

He is the Holy Spirit, Who leads into all truth. The world cannot receive Him, because it isn't looking for Him and doesn't recognize Him. But you know Him, because He lives with you now and later will be in you.
- John 14:17

The Holy Spirit … will teach you everything and will remind you of everything I have told you. - John 14:26

One of the great mysteries of the Christian faith is that God is three beings in one—God the Father, Jesus the Son, and the Holy Spirit. God became human in Jesus so that He could die for our sins. Jesus rose from the dead, demonstrating His power over death and offering salvation and eternal life to all people who believe in Him. When Jesus ascended into heaven, His physical presence left the earth, but He sent the Holy Spirit so that His spiritual presence would still be among humankind. Because you are a believer, the Holy Spirit lives in you.

This Is Promising

We know how dearly God loves us, because He has given us the Holy Spirit to fill our hearts with His love. - Romans 5:5

Q What difference does the Holy Spirit make in my life?

God's Response

We have received God's Spirit (not the world's spirit), so we can know the wonderful things God has freely given us. - 1 Corinthians 2:12

Stephen, full of the Holy Spirit, gazed steadily into heaven and saw the glory of God, and he saw Jesus standing in the place of honor at God's right hand.... As they stoned him, Stephen prayed, "Lord Jesus, receive my spirit." He fell to his knees, shouting, "Lord, don't charge them with this sin!" And with that, he died. - Acts 7:55, 59-60

· · · ———— · · ·

The Christian life is not meant to be a solo journey. You need God's help through other Christians and through the Holy Spirit. God gave you the Holy Spirit because you need Him in order to live the Christian life. Try to do it alone and you'll fail. The Holy Spirit lives in you, enabling you to become more like Christ every day. Only with the Holy Spirit do you have the power to live—or die—for Christ.

This Is Promising
Be filled with the Holy Spirit. - Ephesians 5:18

April

Q

The Bible talks about foolishness.
How can I avoid being a fool?

God's Response

Stop deceiving yourselves. If you think you are wise by this world's standards, you need to become a fool to be truly wise. For the wisdom of this world is foolishness to God. - 1 Corinthians 3:18-19

Yes, a person is a fool to store up earthly wealth but not have a rich relationship with God. - Luke 12:21

The answer to this question depends on whether you want to avoid being considered a fool by God's standards or by the world's definition. The Bible says that a fool does not consider the consequences of his or her actions. A fool never learns from his or her mistakes, and a fool does not listen to good advice. However, when you sincerely try to follow God's blueprint for life, you will have deep inner peace and joy, as well as the assurance that you are making your life count. The so-called wise people of the world may think you are foolish to live this way, but true wisdom is found by investing your time and energy in what will last forever.

This Is Promising

The wise inherit honor, but fools are put to shame! - Proverbs 3:35

Q What does the Bible say about foolishness?

God's Response

Fools have no interest in understanding; they only want to air their own opinions. - Proverbs 18:2

Anyone who hears My teaching and ignores it is foolish, like a person who builds a house on sand. When the rains and floods come and the winds beat against that house, it will collapse with a mighty crash.
- Matthew 7:26-27

Fools are people who ignore God. They are know-it-alls who spout ignorance and could care less about truth. They waste their time, talents, energy, and money on themselves and on accumulating stuff. They don't think about the future—in this life or the next. The Bible compares their lives to building a house on sand; they have no foundation to secure them when the hurricanes of hard times hit. Fools always seem to be in trouble because their lifestyles lead them there. The only sure protection against foolishness is to fear and follow God.

This Is This Is Promising

Those who bring trouble on their families inherit the wind. The fool will be a servant to the wise. - Proverbs 11:29

Q

How can I become wise?

God's Response

If you need wisdom, ask our generous God, and He will give it to you. He will not rebuke you for asking. - James 1:5

Come and listen to My counsel. I'll share my heart with you and make you wise. - Proverbs 1:23

· · · ——————— · · ·

There is an important difference between wisdom and knowledge. All of your education, while important, will not guarantee you wisdom. You may gain a lot of knowledge that will be useful for life and for your future career. However, along with all your knowledge, you need wisdom, which is the proper application of your knowledge. This will give your life meaning and purpose and keep you from making foolish mistakes. If you want to be wise, read and study God's Word. Ask God for wisdom and He will gladly give it to you. Then your choices will be wise because they will include God's perspective. Your education costs you a lot of money, but God's wisdom is free for the asking.

This Is Promising

I, Wisdom, live together with good judgment. I know where to discover knowledge and discernment.... Those who search will surely find me. - Proverbs 8:12, 17

How much do I really need to know about the
Bible? Do I have to read the whole book?

God's Response

*Hilkiah said to Shaphan the court secretary, "I have found the Book
of the Law in the LORD's Temple!" ... So Shaphan read it to the king.
When the king heard what was written in the Law, he tore his clothes
in despair.... "Our ancestors have not obeyed the word of the LORD."*
- 2 Chronicles 34:15, 18-21

To think that you only need to read part of the Bible to know God
is like thinking you can only read part of a good book or see part
of a great movie to know the whole story. King Josiah realized the
importance of this scroll when it was rediscovered in the Temple
(it was lost during the reigns of previous evil kings). It probably
contained the first five books of the Bible that spelled out God's
plan for right living to the Israelites. Josiah immediately knew
that calamity had come on the nation of Israel because they had
stopped reading and obeying God's Word. The Bible is the key to
knowing how to obey God and avoid calamity. The more you read it,
the clearer you will be about how God wants you to live.

This Is Promising

I know His commands lead to eternal life. - John 12:50

Q The Bible is a really old book.
How can it possibly affect me?

God's Response

All Scripture is inspired by God and is useful to teach us what is true and to make us realize what is wrong in our lives. It corrects us when we are wrong and teaches us to do what is right. God uses it to prepare and equip His people to do every good work. - 2 Timothy 3:16-17

The word of God is alive and powerful. It is sharper than the sharpest two-edged sword, cutting between soul and spirit, between joint and marrow. It exposes our innermost thoughts and desires. - Hebrews 4:12

· · · ———— · · ·

Because the Bible is the Word of God, it is the only "living" document. In other words, it is relevant for all people in all places in any time period. It is as contemporary as the heart of God and as relevant as your most urgent need. As God's Word, the Bible is also powerful, but it will not affect you until you read it. Even reading it is not enough, because you need to do what it says. A great prayer to say each time you sit down to read the Bible is, "Lord, open Your Word to me and open me to Your Word."

This Is Promising

The grass withers and the flowers fade, but the word of our God stands forever. - Isaiah 40:8

Q How often should I read my Bible?

God's Response

He must always keep that copy [of the law] with him and read it daily as long as he lives.... This regular reading will prevent him from becoming proud and acting as if he is above his fellow citizens. It will also prevent him from turning away from these commands in the smallest way.

- Deuteronomy 17:19-20

God required the king of Israel to copy the law onto a scroll that he would keep with him and read "daily as long as he lives." Because the Bible is a living document through which God speaks, daily reading is important so that God can communicate with you. It's easy to become distracted and lose touch with Him. Reading God's Word every day keeps you close to the One Who created you for a purpose, Who knows you intimately, and Who can guide you along the best pathway for your life.

This Is Promising

Study this Book of Instruction continually. Meditate on it day and night so you will be sure to obey everything written in it. Only then will you prosper and succeed in all you do. - Joshua 1:8

Q

The Bible is so long and can be boring. What will make it more interesting?

God's Response

When I discovered Your words, I devoured them. They are my joy and my heart's delight, for I bear Your name, O LORD God of Heaven's Armies.
- Jeremiah 15:16

Your promise revives me; it comforts me in all my troubles. - Psalm 119:50

Your laws please me; they give me wise advice. - Psalm 119:24

The Bible is only boring if you expect it to be. You can make your reading exciting by reading smaller portions and taking the time to consider what you read. Try to imagine what it would have been like to live at the time it was written. Try to put yourself into the stories and events you read. Does something in the reading bring you hope or comfort? Is there a promise you can claim? Is there a life principle you can take to heart? The miracle of the Bible is that it has general truths that apply to all people but that also apply uniquely to your specific life. God has written the Bible to everyone, and also just to you. Make the Bible a journey of discovery to see what God is saying to you.

This Is Promising

I have hidden Your word in my heart, that I might not sin against You.
- Psalm 119:11

Q

How can I continue to get something out of my daily reading of the Bible?

God's Response

Ezra was a scribe who was well versed in the Law of Moses, which the LORD, the God of Israel, had given to the people of Israel.... The gracious hand of his God was on him. This was because Ezra had determined to study and obey the Law of the LORD and to teach those decrees and regulations to the people of Israel. - Ezra 7:6, 9-10

The truth is that you will have ups and downs when it comes to reading the Bible. Some days you will feel as if every word is spoken right to you and other days you will feel that you just aren't getting anything. The key is to be consistent and faithful. Ezra knew the Scriptures because he was determined to study, obey, and teach them. As you read God's Word every day, consider what you need to do as a result of what you've read. What change needs to happen for you to be more obedient? Determine to act on what you've learned and consider how God might use you to teach or share what you are learning with others. Knowing you may have to teach or lead by example can really motivate you to learn!

This Is Promising

Teach the law to anyone who does not know it. - Ezra 7:25

Q

The Old Testament has some confusing and gory stuff in it; it's hard to relate to sometimes. What is the value in reading it?

God's Response

All Scripture is inspired by God and is useful to teach us what is true and to make us realize what is wrong in our lives. It corrects us when we are wrong and teaches us to do what is right. - 2 Timothy 3:16

[Jesus said,] "Don't misunderstand why I have come. I did not come to abolish the law of Moses or the writings of the prophets. No, I came to accomplish their purpose." - Matthew 5:17

· · · ———— · · ·

As you read through the Old Testament, you do indeed come across some very strange stories, but some current news stories are equally bizarre and disturbing. One of the great things about the Bible is that it deals with real people in real situations, and this can often be messy. The Old Testament explains how sin came into the world, what the results of sin are, and how God set in motion a plan to deal with sin. The Old Testament points to Christ as the Savior that we need. It is an important and essential part of God's story that applies to you.

This Is Promising

I tell you the truth, until heaven and earth disappear, not even the smallest detail of God's law will disappear until its purpose is achieved.
- Matthew 5:18

Q

Should I be in a Bible study or can I just read the Bible alone?

God's Response

Meanwhile, a Jew named Apollos ... had been taught the way of the Lord, and he taught others about Jesus with an enthusiastic spirit and with accuracy. However, he knew only about John's baptism. When Priscilla and Aquila heard him preaching boldly in the synagogue, they took him aside and explained the way of God even more accurately. - Acts 18:24-26

When you see a good movie or read a good book, it is natural to want to talk about it with your friends. The Bible contains the greatest story ever written, and it is meant to be read and talked about in community. You should keep reading the Bible on your own, but if you have the opportunity to study the Bible in a small group, take advantage of it. You can learn from other believers, gain or offer new insights, and challenge one another to action and accountability. In addition, as with Apollos, there may be things you don't understand that others can teach you.

This Is Promising

I have not kept the good news of Your justice hidden in my heart; I have talked about Your faithfulness and saving power. I have told everyone in the great assembly of Your unfailing love and faithfulness. - Psalm 40:10

Q What is prayer and why is it important?

God's Response

The next morning, Jesus got up and went out to an isolated place to pray.
- Mark 1:35

Don't worry about anything; instead, pray about everything.
- Philippians 4:6

The earnest prayer of a righteous person has great power and produces wonderful results. - James 5:16

We always thank God for all of you and pray for you constantly.
- 1 Thessalonians 1:2

Why should you pray? Because prayer changes things! It changes the one who prays and it can change what is prayed for. Although God is all-powerful and all-knowing, He has chosen to let us help Him change the world through our prayers. How this works is a mystery to us because of our limited understanding, but it is a reality. Why, then, do we spend so little time in prayer? Jesus spent time alone praying to His Father in heaven, modeling the importance of prayer for us as well.

This Is Promising

The LORD is close to all who call on Him, yes, to all who call on Him in truth. - Psalm 145:18

Q How often should I pray?

God's Response

The administrators and high officers went to the king and said, …
"Give orders that for the next thirty days any person who prays to anyone,
divine or human—except to you, Your Majesty—will be thrown into the
den of lions." … But when Daniel learned that the law had been signed,
he went home and knelt down as usual in his upstairs room, with its
windows open toward Jerusalem. He prayed three times a day, just as
he had always done, giving thanks to his God. - Daniel 6:6-7, 10

How often should you pray? More than you do now. Daniel knew
about the law against praying to anyone except the king, yet he
continued to pray to God three times a day. The point is not that
you must pray three times a day, but that you have a disciplined
prayer life, taking time to talk to God daily. As you make prayer a
daily habit, you will find yourself talking to God throughout the day,
sometimes in short sentences as you work or between classes, and
sometimes for longer stretches in a quiet place. Don't let the day's
hectic pace make you forget your prayer time. Pray regularly, for
prayer is your lifeline to God.

This Is Promising

Never stop praying. - 1 Thessalonians 5:17

Q Does God really hear me when I pray?

God's Response

King Sennacherib … sent messengers … with this message … "This message is for King Hezekiah of Judah. Don't let your God, in whom you trust, deceive you with promises that Jerusalem will not be captured by the king of Assyria. You know perfectly well what the kings of Assyria have done wherever they have gone. They have completely destroyed everyone who stood in their way! Why should you be any different? Have the gods of other nations rescued them?" … After Hezekiah received the letter from the messengers and read it, he went up to the LORD's Temple and spread it out before the LORD. - 2 Kings 19:9-14

King Sennacherib didn't think that the God of the little nation of Judah would be any different from the gods of the other nations he had conquered. He was wrong. King Hezekiah wasn't praying to just any old god, but to the God of the universe. Hezekiah knew his God answered prayer, so he took his problem and spread it out before the Lord. You can do the same, knowing that He hears and will answer.

This Is Promising

I love the LORD because He hears my voice and my prayer for mercy.
- Psalm 116:1

Q Do I have to pray in a certain way, with certain words?

God's Response

When I heard this, I sat down and wept. In fact, for days I mourned, fasted, and prayed to the God of heaven. - Nehemiah 1:4

The king asked, "Well, how can I help you?" With a prayer to the God of heaven, I replied. - Nehemiah 2:4-5

We prayed to our God and guarded the city day and night to protect ourselves. - Nehemiah 4:9

Prayer can happen in many ways with many kinds of words. Nehemiah had times of extended prayer to God, sometimes with fasting. He also shot quick prayers to heaven when he needed God's immediate help. He prayed for protection and strength. In short, he communicated with God, and there are many ways to communicate. Use them all as needed. Say what you need to say to God in words or thoughts. The Bible says that "the Holy Spirit prays for us with groanings that cannot be expressed in words" (Romans 8:26). The point is to use many different ways to communicate with God so that you stay closely in touch and express your real thoughts and feelings to Him.

This Is Promising

Because He bends down to listen, I will pray as long as I have breath!

- Psalm 116:2

Q

If I forget to mention something in prayer, does God still know it's on my mind?

God's Response

We don't know what God wants us to pray for. But the Holy Spirit prays for us with groanings that cannot be expressed in words. And the Father Who knows all hearts knows what the Spirit is saying, for the Spirit pleads for us believers in harmony with God's own will. - Romans 8:26-27

You know what I am going to say even before I say it, LORD. - Psalm 139:4

· · · ———— · · ·

God knows your thoughts. That can be intimidating—depending on what you are thinking about—or it can be comforting. When you pray, you don't need to go through your entire list every time. Instead, the Spirit will bring to mind certain needs at certain times that you can bring to God in prayer. That doesn't mean that other prayer items are being missed, however. God knows what's on your heart.

Q

What happens when I don't get answers to my prayers?

God's Response

Jesus told His disciples a story to show that they should always pray and never give up. "There was a judge in a certain city," he said, "who neither feared God nor cared about people. A widow of that city came to him repeatedly, saying, 'Give me justice in this dispute with my enemy.' The judge ignored her for a while, but finally he said to himself, 'I don't fear God or care about people, but this woman is driving me crazy. I'm going to see that she gets justice, because she is wearing me out with her constant requests!" - Luke 18:1-5

The point of this parable is not that we should—or could—wear God out with our persistent prayers, but to make the point that if evil people will eventually answer a repeated request, certainly a loving God will answer our prayers. When God doesn't seem to answer, don't give up! Keep on praying! God has reasons for making you wait, but the Bible is also clear that persistence in prayer is important and gets results. God may give you a "no" rather than a "yes," but an answer will usually come as you persist in prayer.

This Is Promising

Learn a lesson from this unjust judge. Even he rendered a just decision in the end. So don't you think God will surely give justice to His chosen people who cry out to Him day and night? Will He keep putting them off?
- Luke 18:6-7

Q

Should I go to church?
Do I have to go every week?

God's Response

When He came to the village of Nazareth, His boyhood home, He went as usual to the synagogue on the Sabbath. - Luke 4:16

He led me all around among the bones that covered the valley floor.... Then He asked me, "Son of man, can these bones become living people again?" "O Sovereign LORD," I replied, "You alone know the answer to that." Then He said to me, ... "I will put breath into you, and you will come to life. Then you will know that I am the LORD." - Ezekiel 37:2-6

If anyone might have found church a little boring, it was Jesus. Imagine being God and attending a church service! Yet Jesus went "as usual to the synagogue on the Sabbath." The Bible makes it clear that getting together to worship with other believers is essential to a Christian's life. Maybe your church is boring. Maybe it's no better than old, dry bones. Realize that God has the power to bring life even to what seems dead. He also has the power to change your perspective about church. Pray for your church, your pastor, and yourself. Be a part of what's alive—who knows what impact you'll have!

This Is Promising

Let us not neglect our meeting together. - Hebrews 10:25

Q

What is the purpose of church?

God's Response

Each day the Lord added to their fellowship those who were being saved.
- Acts 2:47

The human body has many parts, but the many parts make up one whole body. So it is with the body of Christ. Some of us are Jews, some are Gentiles, some are slaves, and some are free. But we have all been baptized into one body by one Spirit, and we all share the same Spirit.
- 1 Corinthians 12:12-13

The church exists to encourage and equip Christians and to reach out to those who don't know Christ. The church is not a social club, a secret society, or a place to hide from the world. The church is made up of imperfect people who make mistakes, but despite all of its imperfections, the church is still God's vehicle for changing the world. It is not optional for Christians to be a part of the church; it is a privilege and an opportunity. It is your place to grow in your belief, to belong to a loving community, and to become all that God has designed you to be.

This Is Promising

Upon this rock I will build My church, and all the powers of hell will not conquer it. - Matthew 16:18

Q

How should I worship God?
What does that involve?

God's Response

O LORD, the God of our ancestor Israel, may You be praised forever and ever! Yours, O LORD, is the greatness, the power, the glory, the victory, and the majesty. Everything in the heavens and on earth is Yours, O LORD, and this is Your kingdom. We adore You as the one who is over all things. Wealth and honor come from You alone, for You rule over everything. Power and might are in Your hand, and at Your discretion people are made great and given strength. - 1 Chronicles 29:10-12

··· ——— ···

You were created for worship, which is recognizing Who God is and responding to Him in love. The Bible teaches that God alone is worthy of our worship, which can be done at any time and in any place. It can take different forms—singing, meditating, praying, listening intently to sermons, giving, or serving. When you do these things, focused on God and your love for Him, you are worshiping.

This Is Promising

They were calling out to each other, "Holy, holy, holy is the LORD of Heaven's Armies! The whole earth is filled with His glory!" - Isaiah 6:3

Q Why is it important for me to worship God?

God's Response

I am the LORD your God, Who rescued you from the land of Egypt, the place of your slavery. You must not have any other god but Me. - Exodus 20:2-3

We do not think of ourselves as a worshiping culture, but our behavior often suggests otherwise. Consider our weekly gatherings of up to one hundred thousand frenzied fans observing a ceremony of men dressed in strange garb acting out a violent drama of conquest. Others join in at home by way of a small glowing shrine set up in the family room. Or consider how thousands of young people scream and throw themselves at the stage where their rock-star idols are performing. Human beings are created to worship, to give ultimate value to someone greater than themselves, and then to revere, adore, and obey by ordering the priorities of their lives around the one that they worship. The Bible teaches that only God—the creator of all things and all people—is worthy of our worship. Worship, more than anything, will connect you with God, the source of your hope and your future.

This Is Promising

Great is the LORD! He is most worthy of praise! No one can measure His greatness. - Psalm 145:3

Q

My Christian friends all go to different churches that worship in different ways. Is there a right or wrong way to worship?

God's Response

Come, let us sing to the LORD! … Let us kneel before the Lord our maker.
- Psalm 95:1, 6

David danced before the LORD with all his might, wearing a priestly garment. - 2 Samuel 6:14

Everything that is done must strengthen all of you…. For God is not a God of disorder but of peace. - 1 Corinthians 14:26, 33

· · · · · · · · ·

There's as much variety in worship as there are churches in which to worship. Churches may include praise songs with drums, hymns accompanied by an organ, or skits and slide shows. At church you may kneel, stand, or even dance! God loves variety. Of the many different ways in which God's people can express their worship, none is wrong as long as the focus is on God, and the attitude of the worshipers is loving and respectful. Then God is glorified.

This Is Promising

Everything on earth will worship You; they will sing Your praises, shouting Your name in glorious songs. - Psalm 66:4

Q

Right and wrong are not always as clear as black and white. How can I be sure of the right thing to do?

God's Response

Give me an understanding heart so that I can govern Your people well and know the difference between right and wrong. - 1 Kings 3:9

Don't copy the behavior and customs of this world, but let God transform you into a new person by changing the way you think. Then you will learn to know God's will for you, which is good and pleasing and perfect.
- Romans 12:2

You will constantly be faced with making choices between right and wrong. Some choices will be very clear, and then it's just a matter of being strong enough to do what is right. At other times, the choices may not be as clear. That's when you need to depend on God's wisdom in order to know the right choice. The wrong things in life often seem attractive to the human heart and mind, and that makes us vulnerable. Weigh your choices, using God's Word as the standard of truth. Does what you are considering contradict the truths taught in the Bible? If so, it is always wrong. If you're not sure, it is also wise to seek advice from godly people who closely follow the Lord.

This Is Promising

Solid food is for those who are mature, who through training have the skill to recognize the difference between right and wrong. - Hebrews 5:14

Q Everyone says that truth is whatever each person thinks it is. How can I know what is really the truth?

God's Response

Jesus responded, "You say I am a king. Actually, I was born and came into the world to testify to the truth. All who love the truth recognize that what I say is true." "What is truth?" Pilate asked. - John 18:37-38

Like Pilate, many people today—and probably many of your friends—think that truth is whatever they want it to be, but when there is no standard for truth, there is no standard for right and wrong. A society can determine that abuse, deceit, and stealing are acceptable behaviors. There has to be an objective standard that all people everywhere are always meant to follow. Even our own consciences tell us that there is such a standard. The Bible says that truth exists in the person and character of God. He didn't just create truth; He is truth, so only truth can come from Him. All of our choices have both immediate and future consequences. Read the Bible and check out the consequences of living by God's standards as compared to living by your own definition of truth. Then ask yourself which way is right.

This Is Promising

You will know the truth, and the truth will set you free. - John 8:32

Several people I know at school say they're gay.
What does God say about that?

God's Response

Do not practice homosexuality … it is a detestable sin. - Leviticus 18:22

Even the women turned against the natural way to have sex and instead indulged in sex with each other. And the men, instead of having normal sexual relations with women, burned with lust for each other. Men did shameful things with other men, and as a result of this sin, they suffered within themselves the penalty they deserved. - Romans 1:26-27

People often say that God isn't against homosexuality. They claim that the words in the Bible are "cultural" and that God didn't mean for them to apply to today's world. But when God speaks against something in both the Old and New Testaments, you can be sure that His words are not merely cultural. God sees homosexuality as a sin. Different people have different weaknesses. Some have trouble with gambling, lust, lying, or homosexuality. You can't help it if you have a desire to sin in a specific way; but you can help acting on that desire. The standard is the same for all of us—God calls us to sexual purity, whether our desire is for the opposite sex or not.

This Is Promising

The temptations in your life are no different from what others experience. And God is faithful. He will not allow the temptation to be more than you can stand. When you are tempted, He will show you a way out so that you can endure. - 1 Corinthians 10:13

Q How should I treat the people
I know who are homosexuals?

God's Response

You are the light of the world—like a city on a hilltop that cannot be hidden. No one lights a lamp and then puts it under a basket. Instead, a lamp is placed on a stand, where it gives light to everyone in the house.
- *Matthew 5:14-15*

When Jesus heard this, He said, "Healthy people don't need a doctor—sick people do.... For I have come to call not those who think they are righteous, but those who know they are sinners." - Matthew 9:12-13

As a Christian, you are called to be a light that attracts people. You can be a kind friend to those you know who are homosexual, and you can treat them as Christ treated everyone with whom He came in contact. Don't compromise your beliefs, and don't preach to your friends, telling them how evil and wrong they are. If lived as Jesus lived it, Christianity is attractive to others. They will want to know what makes you different.

This Is Promising

Now I am giving you a new commandment: Love each other. Just as I have loved you, you should love each other. - John 13:34

Q Can a person be Christian and be a homosexual?

God's Response

The night is almost gone; the day of salvation will soon be here. So remove your dark deeds like dirty clothes, and put on the shining armor of right living. - Romans 13:12

You are all children of the light and of the day; we don't belong to darkness and night. - 1 Thessalonians 5:5

All believers are sinners saved by grace. True Christians seek to be obedient to God by walking in the light. Since God has clearly stated that homosexuality is a sin, anyone who practices homosexuality makes the choice to sin against God, just like a person who is committing adultery. When people continually choose disobedience as a lifestyle, we may question how serious they are about their Christian faith. However, it's good that God will be their final judge and not us—only God knows a person's real motives and attitude toward Him. Your job is not to judge people, but to love them. You should do what you know is right based on God's Word, and let God judge those who have a different opinion. You can debate and seek the truth with others in order to discover the mind of God.

This Is Promising

Oh, what joy for those whose disobedience is forgiven, whose sins are put out of sight. - Romans 4:7

What does God think about prejudice?

God's Response

[Peter] saw the sky open, and something like a large sheet was let down by its four corners. In the sheet were all sorts of animals, reptiles, and birds. Then a voice said to him, "Get up, Peter; kill and eat them." "No, Lord," Peter declared. "I have never eaten anything that our Jewish laws have declared impure and unclean." But the voice spoke again: "Do not call something unclean if God has made it clean." - Acts 10:11-15

The sad truth is that throughout Christian history, the Bible has at times been twisted and used to promote prejudice and bigotry, whereas the Scriptures really cry out for justice and peace in the world. In this vision given to Peter, God was revealing something startling to Peter's point of view. God was nullifying the Jewish dietary laws to prepare Peter to meet a Gentile (someone who was not a Jew) who was very unlike him and yet a strong fellow believer. God's message in the Bible is for all people. God calls us to treat all people as He treats them—with love, regardless of their race, language, social standing, or skin color.

This Is Promising

You are worthy to take the scroll and break its seals and open it. For You were slaughtered, and Your blood has ransomed people for God from every tribe and language and people and nation. - Revelation 5:9

How can I help when I see others
being mistreated by prejudice?

God's Response

*A Jewish man was traveling on a trip from Jerusalem to Jericho, and he
was attacked by bandits.... A priest came along. But when he saw the
man lying there, he crossed to the other side of the road and passed him
by. A Temple assistant walked over and looked at him lying there, but he
also passed by on the other side. Then a despised Samaritan came along,
and when he saw the man, he felt compassion for him. Going over to him,
the Samaritan soothed his wounds with olive oil and wine and bandaged
them.* - Luke 10:30-34

Jesus told a story about four people traveling on a road: one got
mugged, two fellow Jews passed him by, and a Samaritan stopped
to help. Jews hated Samaritans, so we might have expected the
Samaritan to have also passed by due to prejudice, but he didn't.
When you see people being mistreated by prejudice, be kind and
show the love of Christ—don't pass them by. This could be as simple as a kind word of encouragement, or a harder act of coming to
their defense in a crowd. You may be ridiculed for this, but you will
have the satisfaction of doing what Jesus wants you to do.

This Is Promising

*Above all, clothe yourselves with love, which binds us all together in
perfect harmony.* - Colossians 3:14

Q I know someone who has had an abortion. She seems okay with it, but what does God think about abortion?

God's Response

You made all the delicate, inner parts of my body and knit me together in my mother's womb. Thank You for making me so wonderfully complex! Your workmanship is marvelous—how well I know it. You watched me as I was being formed in utter seclusion, as I was woven together in the dark of the womb. You saw me before I was born. Every day of my life was recorded in Your book. Every moment was laid out before a single day had passed. - Psalm 139:13-16

These words are not just nice poetry—they are inspired words that describe God's creation of each individual. Every person ever created was known by God before he or she was even born. Human beings are not just fetuses until they are born; they are God's workmanship, created by God for a purpose. Human life is God's to create and God's to end. Abortion is deciding to end a human life, and that decision must be left to God alone.

This Is Promising

The LORD gave me this message: "I knew you before I formed you in your mother's womb. Before you were born I set you apart." - Jeremiah 1:4-5

Don't women have the final say about what happens to their bodies? Shouldn't they decide whether or not to have an abortion?

God's Response

Don't you realize that your body is the temple of the Holy Spirit, Who lives in you and was given to you by God? You do not belong to yourself, for God bought you with a high price. So you must honor God with your body. - 1 Corinthians 6:19-20

[Ahaz] offered sacrifices in the valley of Ben-Hinnom, even sacrificing his own sons in the fire. - 2 Chronicles 28:3

Abortion is a hot issue in our society. In certain extreme cases, it is not always clear what to do. However, the idea that women should have the final say about their own bodies assumes that they are their own ultimate authority. The laws of our country have the final say regarding what is a crime and what is not, and God's laws have the final say as to how we live as Christians. As a believer, your body is not your own; you are to glorify God with it. You can do that by having enough control over your body to remain pure from sexual sin. Failing that, and if pregnancy occurs, then you are to glorify God by allowing that child to live. Do not be like evil King Ahaz, who sacrificed his children. Do not sacrifice your child for your own convenience.

This Is Promising

Anyone who welcomes a little child like this on My behalf welcomes me.
- Mark 9:37

May

Q Does God care if I'm going through hard times?

God's Response

"All right, do with him as you please," the LORD said to Satan. "But spare his life." So Satan left the LORD's presence, and he struck Job with terrible boils from head to foot.... His wife said to him, "Are you still trying to maintain your integrity? Curse God and die." But Job replied, "You talk like a foolish woman. Should we accept only good things from the hand of God and never anything bad?" So in all this, Job said nothing wrong. - Job 2:6-10

Sometimes the suffering that comes to us through tough times is not our fault. It just happens. We live in a fallen world where sin is often allowed to run its course, affecting both believers and nonbelievers (Matthew 5:45). God doesn't want to see us suffer. The great message of the Bible is that He promises to bring comfort, healing, and spiritual maturity through it so that we can be stronger, better able to help others, and live with purpose and meaning. As Christians, we also have God's promise that this life is not all there is. We have an eternal future in heaven where God will take away all hurt, pain, and suffering.

This Is Promising

Here on earth you will have many trials and sorrows. But take heart, because I have overcome the world. - John 16:33

Q How will God help me when I'm in trouble?

God's Response

Late that night, the disciples were in their boat in the middle of the lake, and Jesus was alone on land. He saw that they were in serious trouble, rowing hard and struggling against the wind and waves. About three o'clock in the morning Jesus came toward them, walking on the water.
- Mark 6:47-48

I will call to You whenever I'm in trouble, and You will answer me.
- Psalm 86:7

. . . —————— . . .

When you face difficulty, allow God to come alongside you. Don't push Him away. Talk to God about what is happening. He already knows, but He wants you to call out to Him and acknowledge your need for Him. It doesn't matter how large or small the problem is—if it hurts you, it hurts Him and He wants to help. But He won't force His help on you. Ask for His guidance and comfort. Ask Him to help you get through the hard time and to learn something from it.

This Is Promising

In my distress I cried out to the LORD.... He heard me from His sanctuary.
- Psalm 18:6

How can I pray when I'm in trouble?

God's Response

When I was in deep trouble, I searched for the Lord. All night long I prayed, with hands lifted toward heaven, but my soul was not comforted.
- *Psalm 77:2*

I recall all You have done, O LORD; I remember Your wonderful deeds of long ago. They are constantly in my thoughts. I cannot stop thinking about Your mighty works. O God, Your ways are holy. Is there any god as mighty as You? You are the God of great wonders! - Psalm 77:11-14

· · · ———— · · ·

When you're in trouble, pray. Pray when you can't sleep at night, as the psalmist did. Pray with intensity. As you ask for God's help, remember the things He has done for you, the answers to prayer He has given in the past, and the fact that He is the almighty God of miracles. Know that He has helped you and other people of faith before and He will surely help you again.

This Is Promising
I cry out to God; yes, I shout. Oh, that God would listen to me! - Psalm 77:1

Q What happens if I'm in trouble because it's my fault and I did something stupid? Will God help me, or is it up to me to figure it out?

God's Response

The LORD gave this message to Jonah son of Amittai: "Get up and go to the great city of Nineveh." ... But Jonah got up and went in the opposite direction to get away from the LORD. - Jonah 1:1-3

The LORD had arranged for a great fish to swallow Jonah.... Then Jonah prayed to the LORD his God from inside the fish. He said, "I cried out to the LORD in my great trouble, and He answered me." - Jonah 1:17-2:2

If you've done something stupid and gotten yourself into a difficult situation, by all means call out to God. You may not escape the consequences of your actions, but the best place to be even in a tough time is with God. He can take your trouble and work out something good. You will know that He is present and acting on your behalf when you see good come out of bad circumstances. Then learn from it and determine not to make the same mistake again.

This Is Promising

As my life was slipping away, I remembered the LORD. And my earnest prayer went out to You in Your holy Temple. - Jonah 2:7

Q Does God care about my grades?

God's Response

Lazy people want much but get little, but those who work hard will prosper. - Proverbs 13:4

Try to please [your earthly masters] all the time, not just when they are watching you. As slaves of Christ, do the will of God with all your heart. - Ephesians 6:6

Suppose you work in a coffee shop. You're pretty good at it, so your boss asks you to train a new employee that we'll call Tyler. How would you feel about Tyler if he didn't give much effort to learning his new job? What if he just laughed when he messed up an order and made you look bad in front of your boss or a customer? You wouldn't have much respect for Tyler. It's the same with your grades. While you're in school, your main job is to work hard at school. Your grades reflect how much you care about that job and how you work at it. Some kids don't work hard and get As, while some kids work very hard and get Cs. God asks that you give your best effort, develop integrity, and do your best in the job He has given you right now.

This Is Promising

If the master returns and finds that the servant has done a good job, there will be a reward. - Matthew 24:46

Q

Can I pray about my tests and my grades?
Will God help me do well?

God's Response

I stationed the people to stand guard by families, armed with swords, spears, and bows. Then as I looked over the situation, I called together the nobles and the rest of the people and said to them, "Don't be afraid of the enemy! Remember the Lord, who is great and glorious, and fight for your brothers, your sons, your daughters, your wives, and your homes!"
- Nehemiah 4:13-14

We prayed to our God and guarded the city day and night to protect ourselves. - Nehemiah 4:9

You can certainly pray about a test before you take it. However, if you did not study for it, God will not miraculously give you the answers. If you studied hard, you can ask God to give you a clear and peaceful mind so that you can remember what you learned. Nehemiah prayed for protection and then armed the people. Pray to do well on the test and study hard. Usually God won't do for us what we can do for ourselves. When we do our part, He enjoys doing His part, which is above and beyond what we could ever do by ourselves.

This Is Promising

The LORD will send rain at the proper time from His rich treasury in the heavens and will bless all the work you do. - Deuteronomy 28:12

Q

What if I fail a test—or a class?
Is God disappointed in me?

God's Response

Abraham introduced his wife, Sarah, by saying, "She is my sister."
- Genesis 20:2

Then Moses was afraid, thinking, "Everyone knows what I did."
- Exodus 2:14

As Samuel grew old, he appointed his sons to be judges over Israel....
But they were not like their father, for they were greedy for money.
- 1 Samuel 8:1-3

Lots of Bible people failed various "tests." Abraham lied, Moses committed murder, Samuel failed to discipline his sons. That's big stuff compared to failing an exam! If you failed a test because of irresponsibility, you did not work as hard as you should have. God knows that you can do better and expects better work from you. However, you may have failed because you didn't understand the material as well as you thought, or maybe you are just having a rough time—and God understands that, too. Yes, there are times when God is disappointed in us. But God loves you and is your greatest champion. He's always ready to help you be all He created you to be.

This Is Promising

The LORD directs the steps of the godly. He delights in every detail of their lives. Though they stumble, they will never fall, for the LORD holds them by the hand. - Psalm 37:23-24

Q When I've failed, how can I get past it and move on?

God's Response

Suddenly, Jesus' words flashed through Peter's mind: "Before the rooster crows twice, you will deny three times that you even know Me." And he broke down and wept. - Mark 14:72

A third time He asked him, "Simon son of John, do you love Me?" Peter was hurt that Jesus asked the question a third time. He said, "Lord, You know everything. You know that I love You." Jesus said, "Then feed My sheep." - John 21:17

· · · ———— · · ·

Peter had failed miserably. He loved Jesus, but when he realized that being connected with Jesus could put him in deep trouble, he lied his way out. The failure hurt deeply, and Peter probably felt that he was no longer useful to Jesus. He was wrong. Because he humbly repented of his sin, Jesus called him back into service. You may have failed in a friendship, at a test, or in standing for your faith, but failure doesn't mean you're finished. Get up, brush yourself off, ask God to forgive you, and let Him know that you want to be used by Him to accomplish great things.

This Is Promising

Though I fall, I will rise again. - Micah 7:8

Q Can God bring something good out of my failure?

God's Response

People who conceal their sins will not prosper, but if they confess and turn from them, they will receive mercy. - Proverbs 28:13

God's discipline is always good for us, so that we might share in His holiness. No discipline is enjoyable while it is happening—it's painful! But afterward there will be a peaceful harvest of right living for those who are trained in this way. - Hebrews 12:10-11

Failure offers an opportunity to examine yourself. Perhaps a sin still controls you more than it should and needs to be dealt with. Perhaps this failure in one area of life is God leading you in another direction. Don't give in to the temptation to blame others. Instead, put your energy into discovering what God wants to teach you through this. Any discipline you may have to endure can help you grow more mature in your faith, and that should be one of your most important goals.

This Is Promising

God causes everything to work together for the good of those who love God. - Romans 8:28

Q

What is true success in God's eyes?

God's Response

"Son of man," He said, "I am sending you to the nation of Israel, a rebellious nation that has rebelled against Me. They and their ancestors have been rebelling against Me to this very day. They are a stubborn and hard-hearted people. But I am sending you to say to them, 'This is what the Sovereign Lord says!' And whether they listen or refuse to listen—for remember, they are rebels—at least they will know they have had a prophet among them.... But they won't listen, for they are completely rebellious!" - Ezekiel 2:3-5, 7

Those who choose to listen will listen, but those who refuse will refuse, for they are rebels. - Ezekiel 3:27

If you looked at Ezekiel's ministry, you wouldn't say he was a great success. People didn't listen to him, and he seems to have had very little effect on his nation. Yet the Bible pictures Ezekiel as a success because he was obedient to God—a whole book in the Bible tells his story! True success is not how much money you make, how famous you become, how much you accomplish, or even how many converts you have. True success is being obedient to God. When you are obedient, you accomplish all that He wants you to do, and that is enough.

This Is Promising

Our goal is to please Him. - 2 Corinthians 5:9

Q Is it okay for me to want to be successful in this life?

God's Response

This is what the LORD, the God of Israel, says to you, Baruch: You have said, "I am overwhelmed with trouble." … Baruch, this is what the LORD says: "I will destroy this nation that I built. I will uproot what I planted. Are you seeking great things for yourself? Don't do it! I will bring great disaster upon all these people; but I will give you your life as a reward wherever you go. I, the LORD, have spoken!" - Jeremiah 45:2-5

Of course you would prefer to be successful than to be a failure—that's a good thing! But you need to be sure that you have God's perspective on success (see May 10). God told Baruch not to seek great things for himself but simply to be obedient and God would watch over him. Study hard and prepare yourself well for your future. Above all, be obedient to God, and then you will be successful wherever God takes you.

This Is Promising

Commit your actions to the LORD, and your plans will succeed.
- Proverbs 16:3

Q

What kind of success does
God want me to have?

God's Response

*I tell you the truth, anyone who believes in Me will do the same works
I have done, and even greater works, because I am going to be with the
Father. You can ask for anything in My name, and I will do it.*
- John 14:12-13

*You didn't choose Me. I chose You. I appointed you to go and produce
lasting fruit, so that the Father will give you whatever you ask for, using
My name.* - John 15:16

Your greatest success will be in allowing God to carry out His plans
through you. That doesn't let you off the hook, however. What you
learn at school will help you do God's work. If you've been blessed
with the opportunity to gain an education, take advantage of it.
God will make use of your training and your experiences to make
you even more fruitful for Him. Have you been blessed with certain
skills or talents? Thank God and use them to serve Him. God chose
you and created you for a purpose. Often He shows you what to do
as you make use of the abilities and opportunities He sends your
way. Don't let them slip by.

This Is Promising

*Here now is my final conclusion: Fear God and obey His commands, for this
is everyone's duty.* - Ecclesiastes 12:13

Q Why am I here?

God's Response

"I know the plans I have for you," says the LORD. "They are plans for good and not for disaster, to give you a future and a hope." - Jeremiah 29:11

Because we are His children, God has sent the Spirit of His Son into our hearts, prompting us to call out, "Abba, Father." - Galatians 4:6

· · · ———————— · · ·

You are God's child. You belong to a God Who created you for a purpose, and He has plans for you that only you can fulfill. You are here to serve God with whatever time and talent He gives you, and to prepare for living with Him forever. That gives your life great value, and living with that knowledge can make every day a great day!

This Is Promising

I have put my words in your mouth and hidden you safely in My hand. I stretched out the sky like a canopy and laid the foundations of the earth. I am the one who says to Israel, "You are My people!" - Isaiah 51:16

Q Can I know if my life is counting for Jesus?

God's Response

God has given both His promise and His oath. These two things are unchangeable because it is impossible for God to lie. Therefore, we who have fled to Him for refuge can have great confidence as we hold to the hope that lies before us. This hope is a strong and trustworthy anchor for our souls. It leads us through the curtain into God's inner sanctuary.
- *Hebrews 6:18-19*

You may not be able to see how your life influences others on this side of eternity. You may be planting seeds of faith in the lives of people around you that will grow into faith you will never even know about. Instead of trying to have influence, live every day—moment by moment—in obedience to God. The years of life built on daily obedience develop the character and integrity that draw others to Jesus.

This Is Promising
You know of our concern for you from the way we lived when we were with you. - *1 Thessalonians 1:5*

Q Can I really make a difference in the world?

God's Response

[Hezekiah] did what was pleasing in the LORD's sight, just as his ancestor David had done. He removed the pagan shrines, smashed the sacred pillars, and cut down the Asherah poles.... Hezekiah trusted in the LORD, the God of Israel. There was no one like him among all the kings of Judah, either before or after his time. - 2 Kings 18:3-5

Hezekiah was only one man. Sure, he was the king, but many of the kings before him had allowed the nation to slide into idolatry. Hezekiah decided to act on his faith and clean up his kingdom. You're only one person, and perhaps not a very powerful one, but that doesn't mean you have to throw in the towel. All it takes is one person to stand up against wrong, one person to make a difference, one person to take the lead. Maybe you can be the one to "stand in the gap."

This Is Promising

I looked for someone who might rebuild the wall of righteousness that guards the land. I searched for someone to stand in the gap in the wall so I wouldn't have to destroy the land, but I found no one. - Ezekiel 22:30

| **Q** | How can I make the most of the opportunities that come my way? |

God's Response

As for Philip, an angel of the Lord said to him, "Go south down the desert road that runs from Jerusalem to Gaza." So he started out, and he met the treasurer of Ethiopia, a eunuch of great authority under the Kandake, the queen of Ethiopia. The eunuch had gone to Jerusalem to worship, and he was now returning.... And he urged Philip to come up into the carriage and sit with him. - Acts 8:26-28, 31

God had an opportunity for Philip on that desert road. As a result, a powerful man in a kingdom on another continent became a Christian and returned home with the good news of Jesus. Philip may have felt upset at being called away from a thriving ministry, but he obeyed. The next time you find yourself in a situation that is not of your choosing, pay careful attention to God's Spirit. You may be exactly where God wants you and on the verge of a divine opportunity!

This Is Promising

Make the most of every opportunity in these evil days. - Ephesians 5:16

Q

How do I know if an opportunity is from God?

God's Response

Your word is a lamp to guide my feet and a light for my path.
- Psalm 119:105

Be careful to obey all the instructions Moses gave you. Do not deviate from them, turning either to the right or to the left. Then you will be successful in everything you do. - Joshua 1:7

Plans go wrong for lack of advice; many advisers bring success.
- Proverbs 15:22

This is a good question to ask. Many opportunities will present themselves throughout your life, and you cannot and should not follow them all. The best way to know when to take advantage of an opportunity is to stay close to God by reading His Word, praying, and walking with Him every day. The Bible will not always speak directly in favor of a particular opportunity, but no opportunity that contradicts God's Word or leads you away from its principles is from the Lord. You should also pray and seek the wisdom of trustworthy, mature Christians. God will give you peace in your heart regarding the best opportunities.

This Is Promising

I know all the things you do, and I have opened a door for you that no one can close. - Revelation 3:8

Q What if an opportunity looks too difficult? Should I still go for it?

God's Response

I said to them, "You know very well what trouble we are in. Jerusalem lies in ruins, and its gates have been destroyed by fire. Let us rebuild the wall of Jerusalem and end this disgrace!" … They replied at once, "Yes, let's rebuild the wall!" So they began the good work. - Nehemiah 2:17-18

Each time He said, "My grace is all you need. My power works best in weakness." - 2 Corinthians 12:9

Even though the Israelite exiles had been back in Jerusalem for many years, the walls of the city remained broken, leaving its people defenseless and vulnerable. The overwhelming work of rebuilding the walls seemed impossible, but Nehemiah didn't let that stop him. He knew that it had to be done and that God had called him to do it, so Nehemiah made a plan, sought God's help, and mobilized the people. The wall around the huge city was completed in just fifty-two days! Important jobs are rarely going to be easy, but seemingly impossible tasks can be accomplished when God is with you. In fact, God loves to use our weaknesses to show His power, so go for it and see how God works through you!

This Is Promising

Is anything too hard for the LORD? - Genesis 18:14

Q I still feel like a kid sometimes.
How can I be more mature?

God's Response

Don't let anyone think less of you because you are young. Be an example to all believers in what you say, in the way you live, in your love, your faith, and your purity. - 1 Timothy 4:12

Let us stop going over the basic teachings about Christ again and again. Let us go on instead and become mature in our understanding. - Hebrews 6:1

You are still young, but you don't need to wait until you're a certain age to be wise or mature. You can be more mature in your faith by constantly learning—through Bible study and fellowship, by prayer, obedience, listening to older believers, and learning from your life experiences. When you do these things, you will be an example to others no matter how young you are or how immature you feel. Some of history's wisest decisions and greatest accomplishments came from young people.

This Is Promising

When I was a child, I spoke and thought and reasoned as a child. But when I grew up, I put away childish things. - 1 Corinthians 13:11

Q

What can prevent me from
maturing in my faith?

God's Response

*Joash did what was pleasing in the LORD's sight throughout the lifetime
of Jehoiada the priest…. But after Jehoiada's death, the leaders of Judah
… persuaded him to listen to their advice. They decided to abandon the
Temple of the LORD … and they worshiped Asherah poles and idols instead!
Because of this sin, divine anger fell on Judah and Jerusalem.*
- 2 Chronicles 24:2, 17-18

· · · ———— · · ·

You will not mature in your faith if your faith is not of your own
choosing. You can't piggyback on your parents' faith or assume
that just showing up at church is good enough. Chameleon faith
is no faith at all. If you change to accommodate those around you,
you will be immature like Joash, and your faith will lack depth and
strength. If you want to be more mature, follow God because you
sincerely want to and not because someone else is pressuring you.
Don't let your commitment change with circumstances.

This Is Promising

You, dear friends, must build each other up in your most holy faith.
- Jude 1:20

Q

Can I know that God is really with me?

God's Response

Shadrach, Meshach, and Abednego, securely tied, fell into the roaring flames. But suddenly, Nebuchadnezzar jumped up in amazement and exclaimed to his advisers, "Didn't we tie up three men and throw them into the furnace?" "Yes, Your Majesty, we certainly did," they replied." "Look!" Nebuchadnezzar shouted. "I see four men, unbound, walking around in the fire unharmed! And the fourth looks like a god!" - Daniel 3:23-25

I know the LORD is always with me. I will not be shaken, for He is right beside me. - Psalm 16:8

· · · ———— · · ·

It was obvious to those watching that this fourth person was supernatural. It could have been an angel or a reincarnate appearance of Christ. In either case, God sent a heavenly visitor to accompany these faithful men during their time of great trial. That same divine being is always with you to comfort and guide you—even in times of great trouble. If you are a believer, the Holy Spirit is within you, and you have the presence of God at all times.

This Is Promising

He is the Holy Spirit.... He lives with you now and later will be in you.
- John 14:17

Q God may be with me, but I sure feel lonely. Why does God allow this?

God's Response

I am convinced that nothing can ever separate us from God's love. Neither death nor life, neither angels nor demons, neither our fears for today nor our worries about tomorrow—not even the powers of hell can separate us from God's love.... Nothing in all creation will ever be able to separate us from the love of God. - Romans 8:38-39

As you struggle with loneliness, allow it to move you toward God rather than away from Him. God created you for relationships with Himself and with others. If you can trust Him with your loneliness, you will win a spiritual victory by defending yourself against the temptation of the enemy to let loneliness or discouragement defeat you. There are stages in everyone's life when they feel lonely or are forced to be separated from friends or family. God allows these times so we will learn to rely on Him. God has provided the church as a great place to find fellowship with other believers. If you're not attending church—or attending one that does not have a warm, welcoming body of believers—find one right away. This is an essential first step.

This Is Promising

The LORD God said, "It is not good for the man to be alone." - Genesis 2:18

Q Can God help me with my loneliness?

God's Response

Let us not neglect our meeting together, as some people do, but encourage one another. - Hebrews 10:25

We are many parts of one body, and we all belong to each other.
- Romans 12:5

There is one body and one Spirit, just as you have been called to one glorious hope for the future. There is one Lord, one faith, one baptism, and one God and Father, who is over all and in all and living through all.
- Ephesians 4:4-6

· · · ———— · · ·

God provided the best way to avoid loneliness: get together with other believers. As you become more involved in a local church, you can join a Sunday school class, Bible study, or small group. Volunteer to serve anywhere that help is needed. When you join with other people to do God's work, you build friendships. You're part of a body, so seek out the other parts and start working together!

This Is Promising
Don't be afraid, for I am with you. - Isaiah 41:10

Q Can I be sure that I belong to God?

God's Response

We can be sure that we know Him if we obey His commandments. If someone claims, "I know God," but doesn't obey God's commandments, that person is a liar and is not living in the truth. But those who obey God's word truly show how completely they love Him. That is how we know we are living in Him. - 1 John 2:3-5

Now we can tell who are children of God.... Anyone who does not live righteously and does not love other believers does not belong to God.
- 1 John 3:10

What you do shows everyone what you really care about. Obeying God is proof that you love Him and really try to follow Him. Since you are human, you cannot obey God perfectly at all times. Sometimes you will sin and mess up, and God knows that. What He's really looking for is your desire to please and obey Him. That is how God, others, and you know that you belong to God.

This Is Promising

We are both God's workers. And you are God's field. You are God's building.
- 1 Corinthians 3:9

Q What are the privileges of belonging to God?

God's Response

Those who die in the LORD will live; their bodies will rise again!
- Isaiah 26:19

Now that you belong to Christ, you are the true children of Abraham. You are his heirs, and God's promise to Abraham belongs to you. - Galatians 3:29

All praise to God, the Father of our Lord Jesus Christ, Who has blessed us with every spiritual blessing in the heavenly realms because we are united with Christ. - Ephesians 1:3

· · · ·

Belonging to God means that you no longer let sin control you; you can overcome it. You will still sin, but you are no longer enslaved to sin. Belonging to God also means that you can be certain that you will rise from the dead, live eternally with God, and receive all that God has promised His people in the Bible. This includes blessings you can experience today, such as peace of heart, comfort, great Christian friendships, and the satisfaction of knowing you are doing what God has created you to do. These are just a few of the countless privileges of belonging to God.

This Is Promising

Now there is no condemnation for those who belong to Christ Jesus.
- Romans 8:1

Q How do I belong to God and
still live in this world?

God's Response

*The world would love you as one of its own if you belonged to it, but you
are no longer part of the world. I chose you to come out of the world, so
it hates you.... They will do all this to you because of Me, for they have
rejected the One Who sent me. - John 15:19-21*

No one can serve two masters. - Matthew 6:24

You are the salt of the earth. - Matthew 5:13

God could have chosen to take Christians to heaven immediately
when they believe in Jesus. However, because He leaves us here, He
obviously expects those who belong to Him to live in and influence
the world. Many who don't believe in God simply can't understand
why you believe what you do and will think you are a flake. Others
who are opposed to God will actively oppose you. When you realize
that Jesus predicted these attitudes, you will be more patient as you
try to live among godless people. Choose to be "salt"—a positive
witness for God.

This Is Promising

*They were looking for a better place, a heavenly homeland. That is why
God is not ashamed to be called their God, for He has prepared a city for
them. - Hebrews 11:16*

Q Does God's presence in my life affect my relationships?

God's Response

If we are living in the light, as God is in the light, then we have fellowship with each other, and the blood of Jesus, His Son, cleanses us from all sin.
- 1 John 1:7

Don't copy the behavior and customs of this world, but let God transform you into a new person by changing the way you think. - Romans 12:2

Having a good relationship with God gives you better relationships with others. You have unity, fellowship, and the privilege of prayer with other Christians because of God's presence in your life. You will have other relationships with non-Christian friends as you practice using the fruit of the Spirit, such as love, joy, peace, patience, kindness, and gentleness. God warns you not to allow any relationship to compromise your faithfulness to Him. The closer you get to God, the more He will transform you, and the more you will want to obey Him. Then you will love and be loved more by others who love God.

This Is Promising

Two people are better off than one, for they can help each other succeed. If one person falls, the other can reach out and help. But someone who falls alone is in real trouble. - Ecclesiastes 4:9-10

Q Does God's presence in my life affect me today?

God's Response

Because of Christ and our faith in Him, we can now come boldly and confidently into God's presence. - Ephesians 3:12

Now He has reconciled you to Himself through the death of Christ in His physical body. As a result, He has brought you into His own presence, and you are holy and blameless as you stand before Him without a single fault. - Colossians 1:22

When you have a free pass to a favorite event, you don't hesitate to enter. Jesus' death and resurrection are your free pass into God's presence. When you put your trust in Jesus, you can confidently enter God's presence. You can have an audience with the king of the universe at any time regarding anything that happens in your life. That should overcome your worry, fear, concerns, and uncertainties. Anything that happens today, God can handle for you.

This Is Promising

Come boldly to the throne of our gracious God. - Hebrews 4:16

Q Does God's presence in my life affect my future?

God's Response

We have a priceless inheritance—an inheritance that is kept in heaven for you, pure and undefiled, beyond the reach of change and decay. And through your faith, God is protecting you by His power until you receive this salvation, which is ready to be revealed on the last day for all to see.
- 1 Peter 1:4-5

That is what the Scriptures mean when they say, "No eye has seen, no ear has heard, and no mind has imagined what God has prepared for those who love Him." But it was to us that God revealed these things by His Spirit. - 1 Corinthians 2:9-10

God promises Christians that a priceless treasure is already awaiting us in heaven, held until that future time when we leave this earth by death or when Christ returns. If you're a Christian, your future is secure and eternal because of God's presence in your life. Without God's presence, you cannot have an eternal future in heaven.

This Is Promising

Because of His grace He declared us righteous and gave us confidence that we will inherit eternal life. - Titus 3:7

Q

Why doesn't God make my future more clear to me?

God's Response

"When you are old, you will stretch out your hands, and others will dress you and take you where you don't want to go." Jesus said this to let [Peter] know by what kind of death he would glorify God. Then Jesus told him, "Follow me." Peter turned around and saw behind them the disciple Jesus loved.... Peter asked Jesus, "What about him, Lord?" Jesus replied, "If I want him to remain alive until I return, what is that to you? As for you, follow Me." - John 21:18-22

Peter wanted to know his future and the future of his friends. We all wish God would make our future a little more clear so we'd know just where to go, what to do, and be warned ahead of time about bad things. God doesn't work that way. Knowing what's ahead would cause you to miss learning to trust during times of uncertainty. God will make the future clear step by step—with just enough light for the steps ahead.

This Is Promising

Your word is a ... light for my path. - Psalm 119:105

Can I know that I'm doing the right things
and making the right choices?

God's Response

*When Athaliah, the mother of King Ahaziah of Judah, learned that her son
was dead, she began to destroy the rest of Judah's royal family. But Ahaziah's
sister Jehosheba … took Ahaziah's infant son, Joash, and stole him away
from among the rest of the king's children, who were about to be killed….
In this way, Jehosheba, wife of Jehoiada the priest and sister of Ahaziah,
hid the child so that Athaliah could not murder him. - 2 Chronicles 22:10-11*

Jehosheba did the right thing, almost on impulse. She could not
save all of the children, but she could save one. Her act changed
the course of the Israelite nation because baby Joash turned into a
godly king who made many great reforms. What affects your future
the most is what you do right now. Today you can be more obedient
to God, and that is always the right thing to do. If you obey Him
today, you can obey Him tomorrow. Each day, as you live out His
Word, you follow Him in exactly the direction He wants you to go.
Then you don't need to worry about the future because He will be
leading you there. Some day you will be able to look back on your
life and see how God has led you, step by step.

This Is Promising

*Give me understanding and I will obey Your instructions; I will put them
into practice with all my heart. - Psalm 119:34*

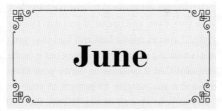

June

Q What priorities should I set with my money?

God's Response

Those who love money will never have enough. How meaningless to think that wealth brings true happiness! - Ecclesiastes 5:10

No one can serve two masters.... You cannot serve both God and money. - Matthew 6:24

· · · ———— · · ·

Spend, save, and give. Those are the three things you can do with your money. Usually we get those activities backwards. The correct order should be give, save, and spend. If you don't set priorities for your money, you'll always spend first and find that you don't have enough. There is nothing wrong with money, but it is wrong to love money to the point that it controls us. Since your money is a gift from God, make it a goal to give 10 percent of your income back to Him—by way of your church or any charity that helps people in Jesus' name. You may not be able to start there, but make it a goal to get there. Then save 10 percent, and use the rest for your personal needs and entertainment. God will bless you for keeping those priorities and you will have fewer money problems.

This Is Promising

Don't love money; be satisfied with what you have. For God has said, "I will never fail you. I will never abandon you." - Hebrews 13:5

Q What is the right attitude toward money?

God's Response

Jesus felt genuine love for him. "There is still one thing you haven't done," He told him. "Go and sell all your possessions and give the money to the poor, and you will have treasure in heaven. Then come, follow Me." At this the man's face fell, and he went away very sad, for he had many possessions. - Mark 10:21-22

When Jesus asked this man to sell everything, it was a test to see what his heart truly loved. This doesn't mean that all believers should sell everything they have. Instead, the point of this story is for you not to allow your money or possessions to become more important to you than Jesus is. He expects you to be responsible about providing for your needs without allowing money to become the central focus of your life. Don't start thinking about how much or how little you have compared with others—this only sets you up for pride or jealousy. Learn to live contentedly within your means while sharing generously with others.

This Is Promising

Yet true godliness with contentment is itself great wealth. After all, we brought nothing with us when we came into the world, and we can't take anything with us when we leave it. - 1 Timothy 6:6-7

I earn hardly any money. Do I have
to give some of my money back to God?

God's Response

You should tithe. - Matthew 23:23

You must each decide in your heart how much to give. And don't give reluctantly or in response to pressure. "For God loves a person who gives cheerfully." - 2 Corinthians 9:7

··· ———— ···

While you may wonder what value the little bit that you can offer God could have, remember that the purpose of tithing is to give you the privilege of participating in God's work. God doesn't need your money—He owns the entire universe. Giving back focuses your attention on God and reminds you that all you have comes from him. A habit of regular tithing keeps God at the top of your priority list and gives you a proper perspective on the rest of your paycheck. Instead of asking, "How much of my money do I need to give to God?" ask yourself, "How much of God's money do I need to keep?"

This Is Promising

Bring all the tithes into the storehouse.... I will open the windows of heaven for you. I will pour out a blessing so great you won't have enough room to take it in! Try it! Put Me to the test! - Malachi 3:10

Q Will God provide for my financial needs?

God's Response

Don't worry about these things, saying, "What will we eat? What will we drink? What will we wear?" These things dominate the thoughts of unbelievers, but your heavenly Father already knows all your needs. Seek the Kingdom of God above all else, and live righteously, and He will give you everything you need. - Matthew 6:31-33

God knows all of your needs and promises to supply them fully. That doesn't mean that you don't have to work hard or take on extra work to meet extra needs. It doesn't mean that you can run up irresponsible debt and expect God to bail you out. You can know, however, that when you're walking in His will, He promises to help in all areas of your life, including finances. If you have been irresponsible, go to God, confess it, and ask for help to change. You will have some tough work ahead, but the Holy Spirit will give you wisdom and the determination to see it through.

This Is Promising

This same God Who takes care of me will supply all your needs from His glorious riches. - Philippians 4:19

Q

My summer job is really boring.
How can I have a better attitude at work?

God's Response

A wise youth harvests in the summer, but one who sleeps during harvest is a disgrace. - Proverbs 10:5

Make it your goal to live a quiet life, minding your own business and working with your hands.... Then people who are not Christians will respect the way you live, and you will not need to depend on others.
- 1 Thessalonians 4:11-12

What if God hired you for your summer job? Would that change your perspective a bit? Well, He has! God has put you in your job—not just to help meet your financial needs, but also so that you might be a witness for Him by how you act and how hard you work. He's undoubtedly preparing you for something more in the future, but He wants to see how you handle things now. See your summer job as God's opportunity for you. God has placed you where you are right now, so find out why.

This Is Promising

Whatever you do or say, do it as a representative of the Lord Jesus, giving thanks through Him to God the Father. - Colossians 3:17

Q

Does God care how I do my job?

God's Response

Whatever you do, do well. - Ecclesiastes 9:10

Try to please [your earthly masters] all the time, not just when they are watching you. As slaves of Christ, do the will of God with all your heart. Work with enthusiasm, as though you were working for the Lord rather than for people. - Ephesians 6:6-7

The desire to work is part of God's character. God worked to create the world, and He gave work to Adam and Eve even before they sinned. Work brings dignity to people because it fulfills an innate desire to contribute something and to make a difference. The way you go about your work also gives you an opportunity to show others what you think about God. When you do excellent work with a positive attitude and care for other people, you model God's character and become a witness for Him. Are you mowing lawns? Honor God by making His creation look beautiful. Are you waiting tables? Serve your customers as though God were ordering lunch. Doing your work well pleases God and makes more of an impact on people than you realize.

This Is Promising

Work willingly at whatever you do, as though you were working for the Lord rather than for people. - Colossians 3:23

Q	Most of the people I work with waste a lot of time. How can I be a good employee?

God's Response

Never be lazy, but work hard and serve the Lord enthusiastically.
- Romans 12:11

Do you see any truly competent workers? They will serve kings rather than working for ordinary people. - Proverbs 22:29

Jeroboam was a very capable young man, and when Solomon saw how industrious he was, he put him in charge of the labor force. - 1 Kings 11:28

· · · ——— · · ·

If you paid someone to do a job for you, you would expect them to do it well. If you were paying them by the hour, you wouldn't want to pay for ten hours of work if you knew they could do the job in five hours. It's no different when someone is paying you to do a job. The Bible says, "Do to others what you would like them to do to you" (Matthew 7:12). Wasting time on the job is stealing from your employers. When you put yourself in your boss's shoes, you can understand why he or she wants employees to arrive on time, do the job well without cutting corners, and go the extra mile. Employers appreciate dependable, honest workers. Working hard, even in your summer job, builds good habits for the future.

This Is Promising

A hard worker has plenty of food, but a person who chases fantasies has no sense. - Proverbs 12:11

Q How can I become more responsible?

God's Response

No accounting of this money was required from the construction supervisors, because they were honest and trustworthy men. - 2 Kings 12:15

The servant to whom he had entrusted the five bags of silver came forward with five more and said, "Master, you gave me five bags of silver to invest, and I have earned five more." The master was full of praise. "Well done, my good and faithful servant. You have been faithful in handling this small amount, so now I will give you many more responsibilities."
- Matthew 25:20-21

Nobody is born responsible. You become responsible by being honest and faithful in every detail of your life, especially in the little things. Missing one number on an address label can send a package to the wrong side of the country. Fudging a few numbers can bring a whole company down and force many people out of work. A loose bolt can cause a car wreck. Taking care of the details can prevent big problems and prepare you to handle larger responsibilities. Being faithful to the small tasks builds up over time to give you the reputation of being a responsible person.

This Is Promising

To those who use well what they are given, even more will be given, and they will have an abundance. But from those who do nothing, even what little they have will be taken away. - Matthew 25:29

Q

What does the Bible say about responsibility for my own actions?

God's Response

It was the woman you gave me who gave me the fruit, and I ate it.
- Genesis 3:12

Instead of hurting [Joseph], let's sell him to those Ishmaelite traders.
- Genesis 37:27

[Pilate] sent for a bowl of water and washed his hands before the crowd, saying, "I am innocent of this man's blood. The responsibility is yours!"
- Matthew 27:24

It seems that no one wants to take responsibility for their actions; it's never our fault. But this is nothing new, as these Bible stories point out. Adam tried to put the blame on Eve; Joseph's brothers put the blame on the traders; Pilate washed his hands of Jesus' death. In the end, each person is responsible for his or her own decisions, behavior, and relationships. You are accountable to others and to the laws of society, but ultimately you are responsible to God. Don't try to pass the buck, but take responsibility for what you do. It will enhance your reputation before God and others.

This Is Promising

Don't be misled—you cannot mock the justice of God. You will always harvest what you plant. - Galatians 6:7

Q

Does it matter for me to have good character?

God's Response

His son Saul was the most handsome man in Israel—head and shoulders taller than anyone else in the land. - 1 Samuel 9:2

The men of Israel saw what a tight spot they were in; and because they were hard pressed by the enemy, they tried to hide in caves, thickets, rocks, holes, and cisterns.... Saul waited there seven days for Samuel, as Samuel had instructed him earlier, but Samuel still didn't come. Saul realized that his troops were rapidly slipping away. So he demanded, "Bring me the burnt offering and the peace offerings!" And Saul sacrificed the burnt offering himself. - 1 Samuel 13:6-9

Saul may have been good-looking, but he had some severe character flaws, one of which was that he continuously disobeyed God. He made unwise, impulsive decisions and directly disobeyed one of God's commands in order to do what he thought was best. His lack of conviction or trust in God would eventually lead to jealousy, murder, instability, paranoia, and his downfall. Character matters. What's deep inside you is far more important than how you look on the outside. What's inside will determine your legacy and your reputation.

This Is Promising

Obedience is better than sacrifice, and submission [to God] is better than offering the fat of rams. - 1 Samuel 15:22

What character qualities does
God want me to have?

God's Response

*The Holy Spirit produces this kind of fruit in our lives: love, joy, peace,
patience, kindness, goodness, faithfulness, gentleness, and self-control....
Those who belong to Christ Jesus have nailed the passions and desires of
their sinful nature to his cross and crucified them there. Since we are living
by the Spirit, let us follow the Spirit's leading in every part of our lives.*
- Galatians 5:22-25

A young, unripe apple falls to the ground in a storm. No longer
connected to the tree, it is cut off from nourishment and will never
become the big, juicy apple it was meant to be. On the ground, it
will rot rather than mature. We are like an apple on the tree when
we remain connected to Jesus. The Holy Spirit will help us and
produce the fruit of God's character—love, joy, peace, patience,
kindness, goodness, and much more. As your fruit matures, you
will get better at obeying God and resisting the storms of life. This
will only happen as you remain joined to Him (see John 15:4-5).

This Is Promising

*When your endurance is fully developed, you will be perfect and complete,
needing nothing.* - James 1:4

Q

How can I love others more?

God's Response

Love is patient and kind. Love is not jealous or boastful or proud or rude. It does not demand its own way. It is not irritable, and it keeps no record of being wronged. It does not rejoice about injustice but rejoices whenever the truth wins out. Love never gives up, never loses faith, is always hopeful, and endures through every circumstance. - 1 Corinthians 13:4-7

We love each other because He loved us first. - 1 John 4:19

Love is a decision to value people with respect, compassion, and courtesy because they are created in God's image. Real love is a consistent and courageous decision to extend yourself for the well-being of others. This applies to all relationships, whether romantic love, family love, good friends, or someone you don't even know who needs your help. As you realize how much God has reached out to you in love, and as you accept His love, you will grow in your ability to love others—even people you don't like.

This Is Promising

Three things will last forever—faith, hope, and love—and the greatest of these is love. - 1 Corinthians 13:13

Q How can I be more joyful?

God's Response

Let the godly rejoice. Let them be glad in God's presence. Let them be filled with joy. - Psalm 68:3

I know the LORD is always with me.... No wonder my heart is glad, and I rejoice. - Psalm 16:8-9

You love Him even though you have never seen Him. Though you do not see Him now, you trust Him; and you rejoice with a glorious, inexpressible joy. - 1 Peter 1:8

· · · ———— · · ·

Joy is your response to that which delights you. The more real and lasting the delight, the more joy you will experience. Nothing could be more real and lasting than a relationship with Jesus Christ, Who loved you enough to die for you and Who offers you everlasting life. Your feelings may go up and down, but real joy runs so deep that nothing can take it away. You know that God loves you, that He created you for a reason, and that your future is set—you will live forever in heaven with no more sin, pain, or trouble. You can be more joyful by purposely celebrating all these certainties promised to you by God.

This Is Promising

Those who have been ransomed by the LORD will ... be filled with joy and gladness. - Isaiah 51:11

Q Is it possible to be joyful even when I'm going through a bad time?

God's Response

Always be full of joy in the Lord. I say it again—rejoice! - Philippians 4:4

Our hearts ache, but we always have joy. We are poor, but we give spiritual riches to others. We own nothing, and yet we have everything.
- 2 Corinthians 6:10

Paul wrote to the Philippians to be full of joy—and he was sitting in prison when he wrote those words! His example teaches an important lesson: Your inner attitudes do not have to reflect your outward circumstances. You can be joyful when going through a bad time because no matter what's going on outside, Jesus is with you and in you. It is only through your relationship with Him that you can find joy in pain, suffering, persecution, and sorrow. That joy comes from knowing that nothing takes God by surprise and that He is in control.

This Is Promising

I will be glad and rejoice in Your unfailing love, for You have seen my troubles, and You care about the anguish of my soul. - Psalm 31:7

Q

Can I feel peaceful in a world that
is anything but peaceful?

God's Response

*I am leaving you with a gift—peace of mind and heart. And the peace
I give is a gift the world cannot give. So don't be troubled or afraid.
Remember what I told you: I am going away, but I will come back to
you again. If you really loved Me, you would be happy that I am going
to the Father, Who is greater than I am. - John 14:27-28*

· · · ——— · · ·

Jesus gave the disciples peace that would help them through their
times of trial ahead. Jesus' peace does not guarantee the absence
of trouble, for even Jesus faced excruciating spiritual, physical,
and emotional struggles. Instead, Jesus' peace supplies strength
and comfort for the burdens you are called to carry and gives you
a rock-solid confidence that your future is secure. The world can
only offer temporary peace in the form of limited distractions.
True inner peace comes only through a relationship with Jesus,
the Prince of Peace.

This Is Promising

*He was pierced for our rebellion, crushed for our sins. He was beaten so we
could be whole. He was whipped so we could be healed. - Isaiah 53:5*

Q Is there any hope for world peace?

God's Response

God blesses those who work for peace, for they will be called the children of God. - Matthew 5:9

A Child is born to us, a Son is given to us.... And He will be called: ... Prince of Peace. - Isaiah 9:6

The LORD will mediate between peoples and will settle disputes between strong nations far away. They will hammer their swords into plowshares and their spears into pruning hooks. Nation will no longer fight against nation, nor train for war anymore. - Micah 4:3

War is an inevitable consequence of human sin. Christians are called to work and pray for peace in the world. Chances are, however, that world peace is hopeless, and sometimes peace can only be obtained by means of war. However, God does promise a time when all wars will stop. You can trust that when Jesus—the Prince of Peace—returns, there will be peace forever.

This Is Promising

Since we have been made right in God's sight by faith, we have peace with God because of what Jesus Christ our Lord has done for us. - Romans 5:1

Q

Sometimes I get really tired of waiting for things and of waiting on God. Will God help me develop patience?

God's Response

Abram was seventy-five years old when he left Haran. He took his wife, Sarai, his nephew Lot, and all his wealth.... Then the LORD appeared to Abram and said, "I will give this land to your descendants."
- Genesis 12:4-5, 7

The Lord kept His word and did for Sarah exactly what He had promised. She became pregnant, and she gave birth to a son for Abraham in his old age.... Abraham was one hundred years old when Isaac was born.
- Genesis 21:1-2, 5

If you do the math in these Bible verses, you'll discover that twenty-five years passed between God's promise and when He actually fulfilled it! No wonder Sarah made a few mistakes along the way, hoping to help God out. God will give you His answers when He's ready, and when He is ready, the timing will be best for you, too. The best way to develop patience is to exercise it. God sometimes makes you wait because He wants you to learn to trust Him in the meantime.

This Is Promising

Put your hope in the LORD. Travel steadily along His path. - **Psalm 37:34**

Q

I know I need to be kind, but it's really hard with some people. How can I be kind even to unkind people?

God's Response

Then the way you live will always honor and please the Lord, and your lives will produce every kind of good fruit. All the while, you will grow as you learn to know God better and better. - Colossians 1:10

Do to others whatever you would like them to do to you. - Matthew 7:12

Your love has given me much joy and comfort, my brother, for your kindness has often refreshed the hearts of God's people. - Philemon 1:7

Kindness is not a single act, but a lifestyle. You practice kindness in all you do and say, always treating others as you would want to be treated. Kindness does not mean always giving in or giving up and letting others have their way. Even when confronting others over a tough issue, you can do it in a kind way without being rude or derogatory. When you do these things, you can have a great impact on others for Christ and His Kingdom.

This Is Promising

Your kindness will reward you. - Proverbs 11:17

Q

How can I be good?

God's Response

The Kingdom of God is not a matter of what we eat or drink, but of living a life of goodness and peace and joy in the Holy Spirit. - Romans 14:17

She must be well respected by everyone because of the good she has done.... Has she been kind to strangers? … Has she helped those who are in trouble? - 1 Timothy 5:10

Goodness is not just being talented at something, as in "she is good at painting." Goodness is a composite of many qualities, such as being kind, helpful, loving, pleasant, generous, and gentle. These qualities exhibit our likeness to God. When Christ takes control of your heart, you begin doing good deeds that, when practiced over a lifetime, will be defined as goodness. When you're growing in goodness day by day and year by year, you're building a reservoir that can become a fountain of goodness flowing out from you to others, showing them what God is like.

This Is Promising

You are a chosen people. You are royal priests, a holy nation, God's very own possession. As a result, you can show others the goodness of God, for He called you out of the darkness into His wonderful light. - 1 Peter 2:9

Q   What is faithfulness?

God's Response

If we are faithful to the end … we will share in all that belongs to Christ.
- Hebrews 3:14

You have been faithful with the little I entrusted to you, so you will be governor of ten cities as your reward. - Luke 19:17

My servant Caleb has a different attitude than the others have. He has remained loyal to me, so I will bring him into the land he explored. His descendants will possess their full share of that land. - Numbers 14:24

Think of someone you don't trust. You don't feel safe about telling them anything confidential. You're not sure if they're really your friend or not; you know they could turn on you. They lack the faithfulness that is crucial to safe and secure relationships. Faithfulness means being steadfast in affection or allegiance. It implies loyalty over the long haul—not just a few times or just when you feel like it. God is the best example of faithfulness as His love is consistent forever, even when we are unfaithful to Him. You can work at being faithful and developing integrity in your relationship with Jesus, your family and friends, at school, and at work. Determine to be known as a faithful person. Start now.

This Is Promising
If you remain faithful even when facing death, I will give you the crown of life. - Revelation 2:10

Q Can I develop faithfulness?

God's Response

Cling tightly to the LORD your God as you have done until now. For the LORD has driven out great and powerful nations for you, and no one has yet been able to defeat you. Each one of you will put to flight a thousand of the enemy, for the LORD your God fights for you, just as He has promised.
- Joshua 23:8-10

To the faithful You show Yourself faithful. - 2 Samuel 22:26

No accounting of this money was required from the construction supervisors, because they were honest and trustworthy men. - 2 Kings 12:15

Faithfulness is loyalty, honesty, and commitment. Decide that you will be loyal to your friends, that you will always tell the truth even if it means getting in trouble, and that you will keep your promises and commitments even if it means missing out on some fun. The more faithful you prove to be, the more opportunities you will be given to show your faithfulness and to handle responsibility for God and others. Someday, when God greets you at heaven's door, He will say to you, "Well done, good and faithful servant."

This Is Promising

Well done, my good and faithful servant. You have been faithful in handling this small amount, so now I will give you many more responsibilities. - Matthew 25:21

Q

Can I be gentle without being a doormat?

God's Response

After the earthquake there was a fire, but the LORD was not in the fire. And after the fire there was the sound of a gentle whisper. - 1 Kings 19:12

He will feed His flock like a shepherd. He will carry the lambs in His arms, holding them close to His heart. He will gently lead the mother sheep with their young. - Isaiah 40:11

A gentle answer deflects anger, but harsh words make tempers flare.
- Proverbs 15:1

Gentleness does not mean being a doormat and letting others walk all over you. God is the perfect example of gentleness, and yet He is also a mighty warrior who is able to defeat the powers of hell. In God's eyes, gentle people are the most powerful and influential in the world because they make an impact without starting conflict or war. Gentleness may be the most powerful weapon in your arsenal. You accomplish more by gentleness than by coercion.

This Is Promising

Come to Me, all of you who are weary and carry heavy burdens, and I will give you rest. Take My yoke upon you. Let Me teach you, because I am humble and gentle at heart, and you will find rest for your souls.
- Matthew 11:28-29

Q

Can I develop better self-control?

God's Response

Supplement your faith with a generous provision of moral excellence, and moral excellence with knowledge, and knowledge with self-control, and self-control with patient endurance, and patient endurance with godliness. - 2 Peter 1:5-6

All athletes are disciplined in their training. They do it to win a prize that will fade away, but we do it for an eternal prize. - 1 Corinthians 9:25

Train yourself to be godly. Physical training is good, but training for godliness is much better, promising benefits in this life and in the life to come. - 1 Timothy 4:7-8

Self-control is one of the hardest character traits to achieve because it means denying what comes naturally to your sinful nature. Some of the hardest things to control are your thoughts, words, and physical appetites. Self-control requires God's work within you as well as your own effort. Take control of your life by honestly assessing your areas of weakness and determining that they will no longer rule you. Stay away from situations in which you lose control, and ask the Holy Spirit to help you overcome those temptations. And don't forget to thank God for His help.

This Is Promising

Better to have self-control than to conquer a city. - Proverbs 16:32

Q Is it sinful when I'm tempted to do bad things?

God's Response

Jesus was led by the Spirit into the wilderness to be tempted there by the devil. For forty days and forty nights He fasted and became very hungry. During that time the devil came and said to Him, "If you are the Son of God, tell these stones to become loaves of bread." But Jesus told him, "No! The Scriptures say, 'People do not live by bread alone, but by every word that comes from the mouth of God.'" - Matthew 4:1-4

[Jesus] faced all of the same testings we do, yet He did not sin. - Hebrews 4:15

· · · ─────── · · ·

It is not a sin to be tempted—Jesus was tempted and He never sinned. Since He faced temptation without giving in to it, He is able to understand and help you when you are tempted. Temptation is unavoidable—what you do when you are tempted is what makes the difference. When you are tempted, do what Jesus did and be ready to respond with the truth of Scripture. Knowing what God thinks is right will help you to resist sin and overcome temptation.

This Is Promising

Since He Himself has gone through suffering and testing, He is able to help us when we are being tested. - Hebrews 2:18

Q

Where does temptation come from?

God's Response

When you are being tempted, do not say, "God is tempting me." God is never tempted to do wrong, and He never tempts anyone else. Temptation comes from our own desires, which entice us and drag us away.
- James 1:13-14

The tree was beautiful and its fruit looked delicious.... So she took some of the fruit and ate it. - Genesis 3:6

I am not surprised! Even Satan disguises himself as an angel of light.
- 2 Corinthians 11:14

· · · ———— · · ·

As a believer, you will face temptation, but it will never come from God! Satan's favorite strategies are to make sin appear to be desirable and good and to twist truth into partial truths. He knows you well enough to know what will tempt you and where your weaknesses are. That's why you need to stay alert, pray, and realize that you are facing a clever enemy.

This Is Promising

Keep watch and pray, so that you will not give in to temptation. For the spirit is willing, but the body is weak! - Matthew 26:41

Q Can I resist temptation?

God's Response

Daniel was determined not to defile himself by eating the food and wine given to them by the king. He asked the chief of staff for permission not to eat these unacceptable foods. - Daniel 1:8

If sinners entice you, turn your back on them! - Proverbs 1:10

· · · ——— · · ·

The time to prepare for battle is before it begins. The time to prepare for temptation is before it overwhelms you. Your greatest defense against temptation is to arm yourself by praying and studying God's Word. Don't fool yourself into thinking that you can resist temptation without knowing the special tactics God provides in the Bible.

This Is Promising

The temptations in your life are no different from what others experience. And God is faithful. He will not allow the temptation to be more than you can stand. When you are tempted, He will show you a way out so that you can endure. - 1 Corinthians 10:13

Q Will God forgive me after I've given in to temptation?

God's Response

The temple was completely filled with people. All the Philistine rulers were there, and there were about three thousand men and women on the roof who were watching as Samson amused them. Then Samson prayed to the LORD, *"Sovereign* LORD, *remember me again. O God, please strengthen me just one more time...." Then Samson put his hands on the two center pillars that held up the temple. Pushing against them with both hands, he prayed, "Let me die with the Philistines." - Judges 16:27-30*

Samson certainly made a mess of things. God had great plans for him, but Samson let his passions rule his life. But in spite of his past, God still answered his prayer. He was willing to hear Samson's confession and repentance and work through him one final time. Often we don't feel like praying after we've sinned. Don't let guilty feelings over sin keep you from your only means of forgiveness.

This Is Promising

If we confess our sins to Him, He is faithful and just to forgive us our sins and to cleanse us from all wickedness. - 1 John 1:9

What's the difference between being tempted and being tested?

God's Response

When your faith is tested, your endurance has a chance to grow.
- James 1:3

God blesses those who patiently endure testing and temptation. Afterward they will receive the crown of life that God has promised to those who love Him. And remember, when you are being tempted, do not say, "God is tempting me." God is never tempted to do wrong, and He never tempts anyone else. - James 1:12-13

You're familiar with being tested—it happens at regular intervals in your classes. You know the drill: Go over the material, learn what you need to know, take the test, give the right answers. When God gives you a test, He's doing it to make you a better person, making sure you learn something you need to know. God wants you to succeed and will never tempt you to sin, which would make you a worse person. Satan, who wants you to fail, is the source of temptation. Satan will tempt you, but God will test you so that you will learn to recognize temptation and avoid it.

This Is Promising

Stay alert! Watch out for your great enemy, the devil. He prowls around like a roaring lion, looking for someone to devour. - 1 Peter 5:8

Q What are some ways that God might test me?

God's Response

It was by faith that Abraham obeyed when God called him to leave home and go to another land.... He went without knowing where he was going.
- *Hebrews 11:8*

Some time later, God tested Abraham's faith. - *Genesis 22:1*

As He did with Abraham, God may test you by asking you to do something hard without giving you all the information you want. He may ask you to do something that requires extreme faith and obedience. As He did with Joshua, He may ask you to do a difficult task in a very strange way. As He did with Mary and Martha, He may wait before giving you an answer to your prayer. Through any test, God is always teaching you more about His own nature and helping your faith to grow stronger.

This Is Promising
These trials will show that your faith is genuine. - *1 Peter 1:7*

Q

Can I know if I've passed God's test?

God's Response

These trials will show that your faith is genuine. It is being tested as fire tests and purifies gold—though your faith is far more precious than mere gold. So when your faith remains strong through many trials, it will bring you much praise and glory and honor on the day when Jesus Christ is revealed to the whole world. - 1 Peter 1:7

. . . ——— . . .

God isn't going to drop a report card down from heaven, but you'll know you've passed His tests when your faith has remained strong in challenging situations. Even if you had some doubts, tears, or fears, if you have stayed loyal to God and continue to do your best to follow Him, you'll emerge on the other side of each test feeling closer to Him because you will have experienced His care firsthand.

This Is Promising

When troubles come your way, consider it an opportunity for great joy. For you know that when your faith is tested, your endurance has a chance to grow. So let it grow, for when your endurance is fully developed, you will be perfect and complete, needing nothing. - James 1:2-4

July

Q Can I be an independent adult
when I'm dependent on God?

God's Response

*I am the true grapevine, and my Father is the gardener.... Remain in Me,
and I will remain in you. For a branch cannot produce fruit if it is severed
from the vine, and you cannot be fruitful unless you remain in Me. Yes,
I am the vine; you are the branches. Those who remain in Me, and I in
them, will produce much fruit. For apart from Me you can do nothing.*
- John 15:1, 4-5

. . . ——————— . . .

As an adult, you are (or will be) independent and making many
of your own decisions. Your dependence on Jesus does not make
you less independent; rather, it makes your decisions good, safe,
and purposeful. Being dependent on Jesus is much like being a
branch attached to a vine—you will get your spiritual strength and
nourishment from God, and this will allow you to make the most
of your decisions.

This Is Promising

*Trust in the LORD with all your heart; do not depend on your own
understanding.* - Proverbs 3:5

Q

What are the dangers of being too independent?

God's Response

I solemnly warned your ancestors when I brought them out of Egypt, "Obey Me!" I have repeated this warning over and over to this day, but your ancestors did not listen or even pay attention. Instead, they stubbornly followed their own evil desires. And because they refused to obey, I brought upon them all the curses described in this covenant. - Jeremiah 11:7-8

Many students can't wait to become adults so they can finally make their own choices and not have to ask their parents for permission to do things. Unfortunately, many use their independence to act in ways that they know their parents would disapprove of, ways that can lead to devastating consequences. As a young adult, don't use your independence to be defiant; instead, show that you are worthy of the title by choosing wisely and honoring God in your choices.

This Is Promising

You are free, yet you are God's slaves, so don't use your freedom as an excuse to do evil. - 1 Peter 2:16

Q What does it mean to be free in Christ?

God's Response

Christ has truly set us free. Now make sure that you stay free, and don't get tied up again in slavery to the law. - Galatians 5:1

The Lord is the Spirit, and wherever the Spirit of the Lord is, there is freedom…. And the Lord—who is the Spirit—makes us more and more like Him as we are changed into His glorious image. - 2 Corinthians 3:17-18

❖ ❖ ❖ — ❖ ❖ ❖

The Bible says that when you believe in Jesus Christ, you become free. This means freedom from all the things in life that prevent you from being happy—guilt and giving in to sin, fear, and addictions. When you are free of those things, you will be free to have a fulfilling life following Jesus, to let go of self and serve God, to live by the truth of God's Word, and to care about others in the way that you really want to.

This Is Promising

You will know the truth, and the truth will set you free…. So if the Son sets you free, you are truly free. - John 8:32, 36

Q

Should I pray for my country?

God's Response

Pray this way for kings and all who are in authority so that we can live peaceful and quiet lives marked by godliness and dignity. - 1 Timothy 2:2

May you hear the humble and earnest requests from me and Your people Israel when we pray toward this place. Yes, hear us from heaven where You live, and when You hear, forgive. - 1 Kings 8:30

When there is moral rot within a nation, its government topples easily.
- Proverbs 28:2

· · · ———— · · ·

Pray that your nation will be protected by God's mighty hand. Pray that your leaders will be humble and wise, able to discern right from wrong, and to champion the needy and helpless. A nation that endorses and condones immorality is subject to judgment and will eventually collapse from the inside. A nation that collectively worships the one true God will stand firm. You may not agree with all your government does, but that doesn't excuse you from praying for it.

This Is Promising

If My people who are called by My name will humble themselves and pray and seek My face and turn from their wicked ways, I will hear from heaven and will forgive their sins and restore their land. - 2 Chronicles 7:14

Q Is it okay to celebrate the Christian life?
Is God okay with celebration?

God's Response

Sing for joy, O heavens! Rejoice, O earth! Burst into song, O mountains!
- Isaiah 49:13

*This day in early spring, in the month of Abib, you have been set free.
You must celebrate this event.... You must explain to your children, "I am
celebrating what the LORD did for me when I left Egypt."* - Exodus 13:4-5, 8

David danced before the LORD with all his might. - 2 Samuel 6:14

When we celebrate, we take time out from the ordinary to honor
and to observe something that is notable, special, or important to
us. Whether we are leaping in joy before the Lord, as King David
did, or solemnly listening to God's Word at the Lord's Supper
(read Luke 22:17-19), we pause to remember, honor, worship, and
praise. The result of all celebration should be joy that comes from
a full and grateful heart. God gives us the ultimate reason to celebrate because He has rescued us from the consequences of sin and
promises us the wonders of eternity.

This Is Promising

*This festival will be a happy time of celebrating with your sons and
daughters ... to honor the Lord ... for it is he who blesses you with
bountiful harvests and gives you success in all your work.*
- Deuteronomy 16:14-15

Q

So it's okay to be enthusiastic about my faith? I thought my faith was all so serious.

God's Response

In fact, it was your enthusiasm that stirred up many of the Macedonian believers to begin giving. - 2 Corinthians 9:2

Work willingly at whatever you do, as though you were working for the Lord rather than for people. - Colossians 3:23

So the LORD sparked the enthusiasm of Zerubbabel … and the enthusiasm of the whole remnant of God's people. They began rebuilding the house of their God, the LORD of Heaven's Armies. - Haggai 1:14

The Christian life is a serious decision, but the decision to follow Jesus brings great delight and joy. In fact, Jesus urges us to serve Him enthusiastically, joyfully, and with a great sense of delight. So celebrate and enjoy every moment of life! Be energetic about what God has given you to do, and do it with all your heart. Your enthusiasm will be infectious!

This Is Promising

Let all that I am praise the LORD; may I never forget the good things He does for me. - Psalm 103:2

Q What can I do for God to show Him I appreciate all He's done for me?

God's Response

With every bone in my body I will praise Him. - Psalm 35:10

Each morning and evening they stood before the LORD to sing songs of thanks and praise to Him. - 1 Chronicles 23:30

The Levites from the clans of Kohath and Korah stood to praise the LORD, the God of Israel, with a very loud shout. - 2 Chronicles 20:19

You can show God your appreciation by praising Him. Sing songs of thanks and praise from the bottom of your heart, and proclaim the glory of His name for others to hear. At school and with your friends, have the courage to tell others what God means to you. A grateful and happy heart is infectious and will be a great witness to the people around you. Think of some of the Christians you respect most. They probably are not shy about joyfully and gratefully sharing what God has done in their lives.

This Is Promising

Let us offer through Jesus a continual sacrifice of praise to God, proclaiming our allegiance to His name. - Hebrews 13:15

Q Why is praise so important to God?

God's Response

Great is the LORD! He is most worthy of praise! He is to be feared above all gods. The gods of other nations are mere idols, but the LORD made the heavens! - 1 Chronicles 16:25-26

Who can list the glorious miracles of the LORD? Who can ever praise Him enough? - Psalm 106:2

Praise is creation's natural response to the greatness of the Creator. It is not unusual for people to burst into spontaneous applause or cheers when a head of state or a celebrity enters a room, and our natural response when we enter God's presence through worship should be praise. The Bible teaches that God created the universe and provides salvation; He alone is worthy of our highest praise. When you consider Who God is and what He has done for you, praise is the only possible response. Jesus said that if people wouldn't lift their voices in praise, the very rocks and stones would cry out!

This Is Promising

If they kept quiet, the stones along the road would burst into cheers!
- Luke 19:40

Q Why does God demand that I obey Him? Isn't that a bit authoritarian?

God's Response

Do what is right and good in the LORD's sight, so all will go well with you. Then you will enter and occupy the good land that the Lord swore to give your ancestors. - Deuteronomy 6:18

The anger of God will fall on all who disobey Him. - Ephesians 5:6

Though He was God, He did not think of equality with God as something to cling to.... humbled Himself in obedience to God. - Philippians 2:6, 8

God's demand for your obedience is based on His commitment to your well-being. Sometimes people have the illusion that freedom is doing anything they want. God says that true freedom comes from obedience and from knowing what not to do. The restrictions are for your good; they help you avoid sin and misery in life and free you to enjoy life to its fullest. Just as a loving parent puts restrictions on a little child to protect him (such as not touching a hot stove or playing in a busy street), God puts boundaries around His children to keep them safe. Disobedience will result in a life full of pain and trouble, and an eternity of misery in hell.

This Is Promising
Do everything as I say, and all will be well! - Jeremiah 7:23

Q

Why is it best to obey God?

God's Response

When [Jesus] had finished speaking, He said to Simon, "Now go out where it is deeper, and let down your nets to catch some fish." "Master," Simon replied, "we worked hard all last night and didn't catch a thing. But if You say so, I'll let the nets down again." And this time their nets were so full of fish they began to tear! - Luke 5:4-6

It didn't make any sense. Jesus was a preacher, not a fisherman. Simon Peter and the other fishermen had fished all night and caught nothing. Then along came Jesus, telling them to try again. Peter knew the fish weren't biting, but something about Jesus' instruction made Peter row back out onto the lake. He was glad he did! The Bible records many things that Jesus tells us to do. If we obey these instructions, we will go through life enjoying God's fullest blessings.

This Is Promising

Don't be afraid! From now on you'll be fishing for people! - Luke 5:10

Q

Does my disobedience hurt God?
Does it hurt me?

God's Response

The people of Israel rebelled against Me, and they refused to obey My decrees.... They wouldn't obey My regulations even though obedience would have given them life.... I made plans to utterly consume them in the wilderness. But again I held back in order to protect the honor of My name before the nations who had seen My power in bringing Israel out of Egypt. But I took a solemn oath against them in the wilderness. I swore I would not bring them into the land I had given them, a land flowing with milk and honey, the most beautiful place on earth. - Ezekiel 20:13-15

When the Bible talks about disobedience, it means a consistent lifestyle of ignoring God or a regular habit of not doing what God says is right. Disobedience hurts God because He wants to give you a life full of good things. Ignoring that means that you don't really care enough to get to know God or see what He has planned for you. It hurts you because when you disobey, you forfeit God's best for you and potentially endanger your eternal future.

This Is Promising

Such people claim they know God, but they deny Him by the way they live.
- Titus 1:16

Q Can my disobedience hurt others?

God's Response

Israel violated the instructions about the things set apart for the Lord. A man named Achan had stolen some of these dedicated things, so the Lord was very angry with the Israelites.... Joshua said to Achan, "Why have you brought trouble on us? The Lord will now bring trouble on you."
- Joshua 7:1, 25

Sin always hurts others besides yourself. Achan sinned, and as a result many men died in Israel's next battle. Joshua questioned God, God threatened to withdraw His presence from the people, and Achan and his entire family were killed. While this story is an extreme example, the point is that your sin always affects those around you. Beware of the temptation to rationalize your sins by saying that they are too small or too personal to hurt anyone but yourself. As a small pebble thrown into a pond causes wide rings of reaction, your sin can cause a wide ring of suffering.

This Is Promising
Don't be fooled by those who try to excuse these sins, for the anger of God will fall on all who disobey Him. - Ephesians 5:6

Q What could happen if I'm disobedient?

God's Response

You disobeyed My command. Why did you do this? So now I declare that I will no longer drive out the people living in your land. They will be thorns in your sides, and their gods will be a constant temptation to you.
- Judges 2:2-3

A prudent person foresees danger and takes precautions. The simpleton goes blindly on and suffers the consequences. - Proverbs 22:3

. . . ———— . . .

When you're not paying attention to God's Word, you expose yourself to temptation. If you put yourself in the path of temptation without the armor of God's Word to protect you, you will probably give in and disobey God. It is a basic life principle that disobedience always leads to negative consequences. Another is that disobedience brings discipline from God, just as a disobedient child should be disciplined by a parent. This is a good thing, for it shows that you are loved. Discipline will help you learn from your mistakes, but it will not erase the consequences you set into motion when you disobeyed.

This Is Promising

My child, don't reject the LORD's discipline, and don't be upset when He corrects you. For the LORD corrects those He loves, just as a father corrects a child in whom he delights. - Proverbs 3:11-12

Q Can I strengthen my faith in God?

God's Response

He said to Thomas, "Put your finger here, and look at My hands. Put your hand into the wound in My side. Don't be faithless any longer. Believe!" "My Lord and my God!" Thomas exclaimed. Then Jesus told him, "You believe because you have seen Me. Blessed are those who believe without seeing Me." - John 20:27-29

Faith comes from hearing, that is, hearing the Good News about Christ.
- Romans 10:17

· · · ———— · · ·

The strongest faith is not based on the physical senses but on spiritual conviction. Though you have never been with Jesus in the flesh like the early disciples, your faith can be strengthened by the testimony of God's Word and by the inner conviction of the Holy Spirit. Like a muscle, faith gets stronger the more you exercise it. When you follow God and see Him come through for you, your faith is stronger when you encounter the next test or trial.

This Is Promising

Jesus said to the disciples, "Have faith in God." - Mark 11:22

Q How much faith must I have?

God's Response

The LORD took Abram outside and said to him, "Look up into the sky and count the stars if you can. That's how many descendants you will have!" And Abram believed the LORD, and the LORD counted him as righteous because of his faith. - Genesis 15:5-6

It was by faith that Abraham obeyed when God called him to leave home and go to another land that God would give him as his inheritance. He went without knowing where he was going. - Hebrews 11:8

· · · ———— · · ·

Faith is not a matter of size or quantity. Abraham believed and obeyed. Did he worry? Did he doubt? Did he second-guess himself at times? Probably. But his radical faith led him to live a radical life that was sold out to God. It is not the size of your faith but the size of the One in whom you believe that makes the difference.

This Is Promising

I tell you the truth, if you had faith even as small as a mustard seed, you could say to this mountain, "Move from here to there," and it would move. Nothing would be impossible. - Matthew 17:20

Q

When I'm struggling in my Christian life and have doubts, does it mean I have less faith?

God's Response

How long, O LORD, must I call for help? But You do not listen! … You do not come to save. Must I forever see these evil deeds? Why must I watch all this misery? Wherever I look, I see destruction and violence.
- *Habakkuk 1:2-3*

I will climb up to my watchtower and stand at my guardpost. There I will wait to see what the LORD says and how He will answer my complaint.
- *Habakkuk 2:1*

Habakkuk saw injustice and evil all around him. He wondered why God did not come to save his nation. Did he doubt God? Perhaps. Your doubts don't mean that you lack faith. They mean that you're human and don't understand all that God does. Take your doubts to Him, knowing that He may not choose to explain everything to you. Let your doubts help your faith to grow; don't let them snuff it out.

This Is Promising

The Lord replied, "Look around at the nations; look and be amazed! For I am doing something in your own day, something you wouldn't believe even if someone told you about it." - Habakkuk 1:5

Q

Is it a sin to doubt God?

God's Response

One of the disciples, Thomas (nicknamed the Twin), was not with the others when Jesus came. They told him, "We have seen the Lord!" But he replied, "I won't believe it unless I see the nail wounds in His hands, put my fingers into them, and place my hand into the wound in His side." Eight days later the disciples were together again, and this time Thomas was with them. The doors were locked; but suddenly, as before, Jesus was standing among them. "Peace be with you," He said. - John 20:24-26

· · ·   · · ·

Thomas doubted, but perhaps we shouldn't be so hard on him. After all, he was being asked to believe that someone rose from the dead! He doubted, but he was still loyal to Jesus and stayed with the disciples. He could have dismissed them all as quacks and left the group forever. Doubt can lead to questions. If the questions get answers that we believed, then doubt has led to belief. It's not a sin to doubt, but don't be content to stay there. Look for answers and you'll find them.

This Is Promising

"My Lord and my God!" Thomas exclaimed. - John 20:28

Q   What should I do with my doubts?

God's Response

John the Baptist, who was in prison, heard about all the things the Messiah was doing. So he sent his disciples to ask Jesus, "Are You the Messiah we've been expecting, or should we keep looking for someone else?" Jesus told them, "Go back to John and tell him what you have heard and seen—the blind see, the lame walk, the lepers are cured, the deaf hear, the dead are raised to life, and the Good News is being preached to the poor."
- Matthew 11:2-5

As John sat in prison, he began to have some doubts about whether Jesus really was the Messiah, but he did the right thing by taking his doubts straight to Jesus. If you have doubts about anything—your salvation, the forgiveness of your sins, God's work in your life—take your doubts to the only One Who can answer. When you doubt, don't turn away from Christ; turn to Him.

This Is Promising

I tell you the truth, of all who have ever lived, none is greater than John the Baptist. - Matthew 11:11

Q If God is all-powerful, why does He allow so much suffering in the world?

God's Response

He has not ignored or belittled the suffering of the needy. He has not turned His back on them, but has listened to their cries for help. - Psalm 22:24

By means of their suffering, He rescues those who suffer. For He gets their attention through adversity. - Job 36:15

Suffering is not a sign that God doesn't care; it is simply a fact of life in this fallen world. If God took away everyone's suffering, we would not need Him or desire heaven. More significantly, we would probably follow God for a magic cure rather than our need for salvation. Some suffering is by chance, such as an auto accident or an illness. Some is a consequence of neglect, failure, or sin. Suffering is a universal experience, and God uses it to draw people to Him. While the Bible never promises a life free from pain, it does assure you that God is with you in your pain and that for those who believe in Him, all pain will one day be gone forever.

This Is Promising

Those who plant in tears will harvest with shouts of joy. They weep as they go to plant their seed, but they sing as they return with the harvest.
- Psalm 126:5-6

Q Life is really tough for my family right now. Does God care about our problems?

God's Response

You keep track of all my sorrows. You have collected all my tears in Your bottle. You have recorded each one in Your book. - Psalm 56:8

In my distress I cried out to the LORD; yes, I prayed to my God for help. He heard me from His sanctuary; my cry to Him reached His ears. - Psalm 18:6

Jesus wept. - John 11:35

Whatever is causing your pain, know that God cares and sends His Holy Spirit to comfort you. Because He cares, He is always by your side, ready to give you power and the strength to cope. He has guaranteed a future in heaven with no pain, and no tear here on earth goes unnoticed. He hates the pain that sin has inflicted on our world. When He went to Lazarus's tomb and saw the pain his death was causing, He felt sad and wept. God cares about your problems. He may not remove them now, but He does promise to help you get through them. Your suffering matters to God because you matter to God.

This Is Promising

The LORD hears His people when they call to Him for help. He rescues them from all their troubles. - Psalm 34:17

Q Can I stay close to God when I'm suffering?

God's Response

Do not be afraid, for I have ransomed you. I have called you by name; you are Mine. When you go through deep waters, I will be with you. When you go through rivers of difficulty, you will not drown. When you walk through the fire of oppression, you will not be burned up; the flames will not consume you. - Isaiah 43:1-2

Jesus suffered, so He understands what you're going through. Trust that no matter what happens, God has not forgotten you. Nothing that happens comes as a surprise to Him. Think about it—He's the only one who knows why the suffering is happening and what He plans to teach you through it. If you stay close to Him, you won't be floundering around wondering. You'll be in the right place to be comforted and taught.

This Is Promising

Come close to God, and God will come close to you. - James 4:8

Q Where is God when I'm suffering?

God's Response

The LORD is my shepherd; I have all that I need. He lets me rest in green meadows; He leads me beside peaceful streams. He renews my strength. He guides me along right paths, bringing honor to His name. Even when I walk through the darkest valley, I will not be afraid, for You are close beside me. Your rod and Your staff protect and comfort me. - Psalm 23:1-4

How precious are Your thoughts about me, O God. They cannot be numbered! I can't even count them; they outnumber the grains of sand! And when I wake up, You are still with me! - Psalm 139:17-18

· · · ———— · · ·

In your suffering, God is right beside you. He never leaves or forsakes you. In the dark valley, He guides you. When you suffer, God draws close, providing a strong shoulder you can cry on, a strong arm you can lean on, and a strong love you can count on.

This Is Promising

I will never fail you. I will never abandon you. - Hebrews 13:5

Q The Bible says that I should fear God.
What does that mean?

God's Response

It was in the year King Uzziah died that I saw the Lord. He was sitting on a lofty throne, and the train of His robe filled the Temple.... Voices shook the Temple to its foundations, and the entire building was filled with smoke. Then I said, "It's all over! I am doomed, for I am a sinful man. I have filthy lips, and I live among a people with filthy lips. Yet I have seen the King, the LORD of Heaven's Armies." - Isaiah 6:1, 4-5

· · · ——— · · ·

Normally, we think of fear as an unpleasant emotion tied to anxious concern or outright terror of being harmed. A different definition of fear can lead to something wonderful. The fear of God is complete awe and respect for Him, and a realization that everything He says about love and justice is true. To fear the Lord is to recognize that God is holy, almighty, righteous, all-knowing, and wise. When you regard God correctly, you gain a clearer picture of yourself as sinful, weak, and needy. The only response to a God Who loves you as you are is to fall at His feet in humble respect. Isaiah recognized his sinfulness before the God Who holds the power of life and death in His hands. His example encourages us to never take God's love and presence in our lives for granted.

This Is Promising

He shows mercy from generation to generation to all who fear Him.
- Luke 1:50

Q What is God's power like?

God's Response

He will answer him from His holy heaven and rescue him by His great power. Some nations boast of their chariots and horses, but we boast in the name of the LORD our God. - Psalm 20:6-7

Jesus got into the boat and started across the lake with His disciples. Suddenly, a fierce storm struck the lake.... The disciples went and woke Him up, shouting, "Lord, save us! We're going to drown!" Jesus responded, "Why are you afraid? You have so little faith!" Then He got up and rebuked the wind and waves, and suddenly all was calm. The disciples were amazed. "Who is this man?" they asked. "Even the winds and waves obey Him!"
- Matthew 8:23-27

Imagine the earth's strongest earthquake, tallest tsunami, wildest volcano, and most devastating hurricane—all in one place. This cannot even begin to compare to God's power, because He is the creator of all these phenomena, and what is created is never more powerful than the creator. This same God, Who instantly calmed the storm over Galilee, has the power to calm the storms in your heart, dry up your flood of fear, quench the fires of lust, and control the whirlwind of your life. Do you believe in God's power, or will you insist on taking matters into your own hands?

This Is Promising

As for me, I will sing about Your power. - Psalm 59:16

Q Can I experience God's power in my life?

God's Response

A final word: Be strong in the Lord and in His mighty power. Put on all of God's armor so that you will be able to stand firm against all strategies of the devil. For we are not fighting against flesh-and-blood enemies, but against evil rulers and authorities of the unseen world, against mighty powers in this dark world, and against evil spirits in the heavenly places.
- Ephesians 6:10-12

God's power comes from His presence within you. The Holy Spirit literally dwells within you, so His power is available to you. You have the power to fight all the battles that come your way—whatever the world brings or Satan sends. Put on God's armor so that you have God's power to fight and win for him.

This Is Promising

This is the secret: Christ lives in you. This gives you assurance of sharing His glory.... I work and struggle so hard, depending on Christ's mighty power that works within me. - Colossians 1:27-29

Q How can I please God?

God's Response

But Moses protested to God, "Who am I to appear before Pharaoh? Who am I to lead the people of Israel out of Egypt?" God answered, "I will be with you." - Exodus 3:11-12

Moses protested again, "What if they won't believe me or listen to me? What if they say, 'The LORD never appeared to you'?" - Exodus 4:1

Moses pleaded with the LORD, "O Lord, I'm not very good with words. I never have been, and I'm not now, even though You have spoken to me. I get tongue-tied, and my words get tangled." - Exodus 4:10

You can please God by refusing to make excuses when He asks you to serve Him. Even the great leader Moses made excuses and upset God by his unwillingness to serve. We all make excuses—we're afraid, too busy, not qualified, too tired. But when God places a need before you and impresses it on your mind, chances are He is calling you to step forward and help meet that need. Step out and watch God do great things through you.

This Is Promising

Be strong and courageous! Do not be afraid and do not panic before them. For the Lord your God will personally go ahead of you. He will neither fail you nor abandon you. - Deuteronomy 31:6

Q Does God forgive me when I disappoint Him?

God's Response

The LORD became angry with Moses. "All right," He said. "What about your brother, Aaron the Levite? I know he speaks well.... Talk to him, and put the words in his mouth. I will be with both of you as you speak, and I will instruct you both in what to do." - Exodus 4:14-15

Moses climbed the mountain to appear before God. - Exodus 19:3

. . . —————— . . .

God had a task for Moses, and Moses didn't want it. God finally agreed to let Aaron go along and speak for Moses, whose feelings of inadequacy were so strong that he could not trust God to help him. But give Moses some credit—he still stepped out and followed where God led. God forgave Moses' lack of trust and used him greatly. Moses needed his brother to go along for a shot of self-confidence, but he went, and God used him to rescue an entire nation from slavery. When you know your sins have disappointed God, don't give up. Keep stepping out toward God, Who will forgive you and continue to work through you, often in marvelous ways.

This Is Promising

You offer forgiveness, that we might learn to fear You. - Psalm 130:4

Q What is grace and how do I receive it?

God's Response

Sin is no longer your master, for you no longer live under the requirements of the law. Instead, you live under the freedom of God's grace. - Romans 6:14

God saved you by His grace when you believed. And you can't take credit for this; it is a gift from God. Salvation is not a reward for the good things we have done, so none of us can boast about it. - Ephesians 2:8-9

Grace is another word for the amazing kindness God showers on us even when we do not deserve it. God's greatest act of kindness is offering us salvation and eternal life, even though we have ignored, neglected, and rebelled against Him. God's grace sets you free from the power of sin when He forgives you, so that each day you can make the choice to overpower your sinful nature. God's grace changes your life because you understand what it feels like to be loved even though you have not loved in return. This should cause you to love others in the same way that God loves you. To whom can you show God's grace today?

This Is Promising

All of this is for your benefit. And as God's grace reaches more and more people, there will be great thanksgiving, and God will receive more and more glory. - 2 Corinthians 4:15

Q Why does God show me mercy?

God's Response

He saved us, not because of the righteous things we had done, but because of His mercy. He washed away our sins, giving us a new birth and new life through the Holy Spirit. - Titus 3:5

Await the mercy of our Lord Jesus Christ, Who will bring you eternal life. In this way, you will keep yourselves safe in God's love. - Jude 1:21

You, O Lord, are a God of compassion and mercy, slow to get angry and filled with unfailing love and faithfulness. - Psalm 86:15

· · · ———— · · ·

You really mess up big at your job and you know your boss is going to be furious. But when he finds out, he says, "That's okay; everyone makes mistakes. I know you're trying hard and will do better next time." He gives you a big break; in other words, he shows you mercy, and that's one of the best feelings in the world. The world can be a bad enough place sometimes, but without mercy it would be unbearable. God gives us mercy every day when we sin in some way and mess up before Him. But if we're sorry, He forgives us and shows us mercy 24–7, 365 days a year. God is the only boss who is that patient! Receive His mercy with a grateful heart.

This Is Promising

Answer my prayers, O LORD, for Your unfailing love is wonderful. Take care of me, for Your mercy is so plentiful. - Psalm 69:16

Q

How does God show me His mercy?

God's Response

He forgives all my sins.... He redeems me from death.... He fills my life with good things. - Psalm 103:3-5

The God of compassion and mercy! I am slow to anger and filled with unfailing love and faithfulness. - Exodus 34:6

God is so rich in mercy, and He loved us so much, that even though we were dead because of our sins, He gave us life. - Ephesians 2:4-5

Mercy has been defined as "not giving a person the punishment he or she deserves." God showers mercy on you each day. He is slow to get angry over your sins, He offers you a way out from the eternal consequences of sin, and He shows you unfailing love no matter what you have done. When you pray for forgiveness, you ask for what you do not deserve, but God gives it to you anyway. It's almost too good to believe, but when you take this step and trust in God's mercy, you'll experience it every day.

This Is Promising

Once you had no identity as a people; now you are God's people. Once you received no mercy; now you have received God's mercy. - 1 Peter 2:10

Q How can I show mercy and compassion to others?

God's Response

Since God chose you to be the holy people He loves, you must clothe yourselves with tenderhearted mercy, kindness, humility, gentleness, and patience. Make allowance for each other's faults, and forgive anyone who offends you. Remember, the Lord forgave you, so you must forgive others.
- Colossians 3:12-13

Shouldn't you have mercy on your fellow servant, just as I had mercy on you? - Matthew 18:33

God's mercy toward us shows us how we should extend mercy to others. Be quick to forgive, to be kind, to be generous in love—even when others don't deserve it. A willingness to show mercy and compassion toward others shows that you understand and appreciate the mercy and compassion God has shown you. It cost Him the life of His Son. What will it cost you to show some mercy and compassion today?

This Is Promising

No, O people, the Lord has told you what is good, and this is what He requires of you: to do what is right, to love mercy, and to walk humbly with your God. - Micah 6:8

August

Q

How can I be more understanding when people around me have needs?

God's Response

"I was hungry, and you fed Me. I was thirsty, and you gave Me a drink. I was a stranger, and you invited Me into your home. I was naked, and you gave me clothing. I was sick, and you cared for Me. I was in prison, and you visited Me." Then these righteous ones will reply, "Lord, when did we ever … ?" And the King will say, "I tell you the truth, when you did it to one of the least of these My brothers and sisters, you were doing it to Me!"
- Matthew 25:35-37, 40

This parable describes acts of mercy you could do every day. You don't have to be a super-Christian, be wealthy, or have special spiritual gifts in order to be kind. You can be more understanding if you look at each person as if he or she were Jesus.

This Is Promising

Share each other's burdens, and in this way obey the law of Christ.
- Galatians 6:2

Q Can I help with people's needs when I'm just one person?

God's Response

Paul's nephew—his sister's son—heard of their plan and went to the fortress and told Paul.... The commander took his hand, led him aside, and asked, "What is it you want to tell me?" Paul's nephew told him, "Some Jews are going to ask you to bring Paul before the high council tomorrow, pretending they want to get some more information. But don't do it! There are more than forty men hiding along the way ready to ambush him. They have vowed not to eat or drink anything until they have killed him. They are ready now, just waiting for your consent."
- Acts 23:16, 19-21

You're just one person, but you may be the only person who can help, and if you don't do it, it may not get done. Paul's nephew saved his life by simply reporting what he overheard. Consider a time when you needed help and one person came through for you. How important was just one person then? When you see a need, do your best to meet it. You may be the only one who can, or who will.

This Is Promising

Their insults have broken my heart, and I am in despair. If only one person would show some pity; if only one would turn and comfort me. - Psalm 69:20

Q Can I have an impact on my community?

God's Response

The whole law can be summed up in this one command: "Love your neighbor as yourself." - Galatians 5:14

Owe nothing to anyone—except for your obligation to love one another. If you love your neighbor, you will fulfill the requirements of God's law.
- Romans 13:8

Be careful to live properly among your unbelieving neighbors. Then even if they accuse you of doing wrong, they will see your honorable behavior, and they will give honor to God when He judges the world. - 1 Peter 2:12

You can have the greatest effect on your community by genuinely loving others, serving them, and remaining faithful to God. It sounds simple, but it actually takes a lot of effort. It's much easier to be selfish and do things to please yourself, but you won't have a good reputation if you consistently live in a selfish way. If your actions and words reflect Jesus to others, even hostile people will end up praising God and respecting you. You will be refreshing to those around you and they will be drawn to you. You may be the only Christian they know—be a good example of Christ to them.

This Is Promising

You are a holy people, who belong to the LORD your God. - Deuteronomy 7:6

Q Can I stay strong in times of trouble?

God's Response

You can be sure of this: The LORD set apart the godly for Himself. The LORD will answer when I call to Him. - Psalm 4:3

Listen to my voice in the morning, LORD. Each morning I bring my requests to You and wait expectantly. - Psalm 5:3

You find out how strong your faith is when trouble comes. Are you really able to put your trust completely in God, or do you accuse Him and become angry with Him? You can stay strong if you learn to look at these times as God's way of drawing you closer to Him. You will feel closest to God during times of trouble because that is when you will cling to Him. He is always there, waiting to answer when you call to Him.

This Is Promising

If we endure hardship, we will reign with Him. If we deny Him, He will deny us. - 2 Timothy 2:12

Q   Why do I often feel like an outsider?

God's Response

Dear friends, I warn you as "temporary residents and foreigners" to keep away from worldly desires that wage war against your very souls.
- 1 Peter 2:11

Don't copy the behavior and customs of this world, but let God transform you into a new person by changing the way you think. - Romans 12:2

I am only a foreigner in the land. Don't hide Your commands from me!
- Psalm 119:19

Chances are that you will feel like an outsider at times. In reality, you are an outsider because your real home is heaven. As a Christian, you know in your heart that things aren't all right on earth now—life was not meant to include crime, violence, backbiting, hatred, power grabbing, lying, and cheating. Someday God will make everything right again and you'll feel at home. In the meantime, keep your relationship with Jesus as top priority; only then will you have the proper perspective about earth right now.

This Is Promising

What blessings await you when people hate you and exclude you and mock you and curse you as evil because you follow the Son of Man. - Luke 6:22

What does it mean to be holy and
live a holy life?

God's Response

*I am writing to … you who have been called by God to be His own holy
people. He made you holy by means of Christ Jesus, just as He did for all
people everywhere who call on the name of our Lord Jesus Christ.*
- 1 Corinthians 1:2

*You were cleansed; you were made holy; you were made right with God by
calling on the name of the Lord Jesus Christ and by the Spirit of our God.*
- 1 Corinthians 6:11

*I plead with you to give your bodies to God because of all He has done
for you. Let them be a living and holy sacrifice—the kind He will find
acceptable.* - Romans 12:1

Think of holiness as both a journey and a destination. To be completely holy is to be sinless, pure, and perfect before God. Of course,
none of us is perfect, so that is our ultimate goal for when we stand
before God in heaven. Holiness also means being set apart by God
for a specific purpose. We are meant to be different from the rest of
the world, and in our life journeys, we hope to become a little more
pure and sinless each day. If you strive to be holy in your earthly
life, you will one day arrive at your final destination to stand as holy
before God.

This Is Promising

You must be holy because I, the LORD your God, am holy. - Leviticus 19:2

Q How is it possible for me to be holy?

God's Response

Through the death of Christ in His physical body … He has brought you into His own presence, and you are holy and blameless as you stand before Him without a single fault. - Colossians 1:22

Even before He made the world, God loved us and chose us in Christ to be holy and without fault in His eyes. - Ephesians 1:4

Christ made us … pure and holy. - 1 Corinthians 1:30

When you became a Christian, God made you holy by forgiving your sins. He looks at you as though you had never sinned, but while He sees you as holy, you are not perfect. You must still work each day to become more like Jesus, because that is our goal on earth. You become sanctified—made holy—through believing and obeying the Word of God. Daily application of the Bible has a purifying effect on our minds and hearts. You grow toward holiness, but you will only be completely holy when you get to heaven.

This Is Promising

I, the LORD, am holy, and I make you holy. - Leviticus 21:8

Q

Is it okay to have desires in my life?

God's Response

That night the LORD appeared to Solomon in a dream, and God said, "What do you want? Ask, and I will give it to you!" - 1 Kings 3:5

Hope deferred makes the heart sick, but a dream fulfilled is a tree of life. - Proverbs 13:12

I desire You more than anything on earth. - Psalm 73:25

May He grant your heart's desires and make all your plans succeed. - Psalm 20:4

All of us are created with a capacity for desire. Desires can be healthy or unhealthy, godly or ungodly, good or bad, casual or intense. Desire is good and healthy if: (1) you don't seek something sinful; (2) it does not become more important than your desire to love and please God; (3) it helps you develop focus and enthusiasm; and (4) it blesses others and honors God. The Bible says that our greatest desire should be to love, follow, please, and obey the Lord. Develop that desire. The more you know Him, the more you will desire Him.

This Is Promising

If you look for Me wholeheartedly, you will find me. - Jeremiah 29:13

Q

How do I know if my desires are right or wrong?

God's Response

One day when Samson was in Timnah, one of the Philistine women caught his eye. When he returned home, he told his father and mother, "A young Philistine woman in Timnah caught my eye. I want to marry her. Get her for me." His father and mother objected. "Isn't there even one woman in our tribe or among all the Israelites you could marry?" they asked. "Why must you go to the pagan Philistines to find a wife?" But Samson told his father, "Get her for me! She looks good to me." - Judges 14:1-3

Fix your thoughts on what is true, and honorable, and right, and pure, and lovely, and admirable. Think about things that are excellent and worthy of praise. - Philippians 4:8

Sinful, selfish desires are very powerful. The desire to get what you want is so strong that it can keep you from thinking straight. When Samson saw the beautiful woman, it was as if his brain froze and he couldn't even think about how bad that relationship would obviously be. There was no way it could work! Like Samson, you can become so obsessed with what you want that you forget to ask if it is what God wants. Make sure that the object of your desire is good, consistent with God's Word, and not harmful to others.

This Is Promising

Wisdom is far more valuable than rubies. Nothing you desire can compare with it. - Proverbs 8:11

Q

Can I develop more of a desire for God?

God's Response

If you only knew the gift God has for you and Who you are speaking to, you would ask Me, and I would give you living water.... Anyone who drinks this water will soon become thirsty again. But those who drink the water I give will never be thirsty again. It becomes a fresh, bubbling spring within them, giving them eternal life. - John 4:10, 13-14

Jesus replied, "I am the bread of life. Whoever comes to Me will never be hungry again." - John 6:35

Even if you could buy anything you wanted, that would not satisfy the deepest longings of your heart. If you won every award in your field of interest, your heart would still not be fulfilled. How can this be? God created you to have a relationship with Him. Until you understand that and pursue Him, your heart will ache. God did not create you to live in a sinful world separate from Him, but in a perfect world side by side with Him. As you get to know Him, this becomes clear, and you will begin to long for eternal life with Him in the perfect world (heaven). Develop a desire for God by drawing close to Him in prayer and Bible reading. Notice His care for you throughout your day. You will sense His nearness—and that will make you desire Him more.

This Is Promising

As the deer longs for streams of water, so I long for You, O God. - Psalm 42:1

Q What kind of power can a Christian really have?

God's Response

I was given a thorn in my flesh, a messenger from Satan to torment me and keep me from becoming proud. Three different times I begged the Lord to take it away. Each time he said, "My grace is all you need. My power works best in weakness." So now I am glad to boast about my weaknesses, so that the power of Christ can work through me. That's why I take pleasure in my weaknesses, and in the insults, hardships, persecutions, and troubles that I suffer for Christ. For when I am weak, then I am strong.
- 2 Corinthians 12:7-10

. . . ———— . . .

Most people think of power as controlling others as the way to get ahead. Jesus says that power comes in serving others and that His power works best through our weaknesses. When God works through our weaknesses, it is clear that He is doing the work, making much more power available to you than when you try to do things by yourself. When you let Jesus take your weaknesses and transform them, you are living with true power.

This Is Promising

We now have this light shining in our hearts, but we ourselves are like fragile clay jars containing this great treasure. This makes it clear that our great power is from God, not from ourselves. - 2 Corinthians 4:7

Q

Can I have more of God's power working in me?

God's Response

Yes, I am the vine; you are the branches. Those who remain in Me, and I in them, will produce much fruit. For apart from Me you can do nothing.
- John 15:5

When Simon saw that the Spirit was given when the apostles laid their hands on people, he offered them money to buy this power…. But Peter replied, "May your money be destroyed with you for thinking God's gift can be bought! You can have no part in this, for your heart is not right with God." - Acts 8:18-21

Spiritual power comes from living closely with Jesus Christ—only then does He make His power available to you. God's power cannot be bought or used for selfish purposes. God gives power for godly living and for helping you do the tasks to which He calls you.

This Is Promising

May you experience the love of Christ, though it is too great to understand fully. Then you will be made complete with all the fullness of life and power that comes from God. - Ephesians 3:19

Does God prepare me for what
He has in store for me?

God's Response

*When her son was born, she named him Samson. And the LORD blessed
him as he grew up.... The Spirit of the LORD began to stir him.... One day
Samson went to the Philistine town of Gaza and spent the night with a
prostitute.... He didn't realize the LORD had left him. So the Philistines
captured him. - Judges 13:24-25; 16:1, 20-21*

*If you keep yourself pure, you will be a special utensil for honorable use.
Your life will be clean, and you will be ready for the Master to use you for
every good work. - 2 Timothy 2:21*

As soon as Samson was born, God's Spirit began to work in him to
get his attention. God wanted to prepare Samson for his unique
work, but Samson was supposed to do his part in return—listen for
God's voice, obey His clear instructions, and act on the opportunities
God would bring him. Sadly, Samson didn't do these things and never reached his full potential. What is the Spirit of the Lord preparing
you for? The key to recognizing His work in your life is to obey God's
clear instructions for living as found in the Bible. If you follow God
in simple obedience, you will walk through the doors of opportunity
that He opens for you.

This Is Promising

*Study this Book of Instruction continually. Meditate on it day and night so
you will be sure to obey everything written in it. Only then will you prosper
and succeed in all you do. - Joshua 1:8*

Q I'm excited about the coming school year, but also a little scared. How can I handle my feelings of insecurity?

God's Response

I pray that from His glorious, unlimited resources He will empower you with inner strength through His Spirit. Then Christ will make His home in your hearts as you trust in Him. Your roots will grow down into God's love and keep you strong. And may you have the power to understand, as all God's people should, how wide, how long, how high, and how deep His love is. - Ephesians 3:16-18

Whether you're at the same school you've always attended or heading off to a new place, you may feel insecure and unsure of yourself. Know that wherever you go, God goes with you and helps you. Take one day at a time. Do your work, be a friend to everyone, enjoy the fun parts, and before you know it, the school year will be over.

This Is Promising

You will be made complete with all the fullness of life and power that comes from God.... Through His mighty power at work within us, to accomplish infinitely more than we might ask or think. - Ephesians 3:19-20

Q Will God help me feel more secure?

God's Response

Moses my servant is dead. Therefore, the time has come for you to lead these people, the Israelites, across the Jordan River into the land I am giving them.... Be strong and very courageous. Be careful to obey all the instructions Moses gave you. Do not deviate from them, turning either to the right or to the left. Then you will be successful in everything you do. Study this Book of Instruction continually. Meditate on it day and night so you will be sure to obey everything written in it. Only then will you prosper and succeed in all you do.... Do not be afraid or discouraged. For the LORD your God is with you wherever you go. - Joshua 1:1-2, 7-9

· · · ——— · · ·

When Moses died, Joshua became Israel's new leader. He probably felt a bit insecure; after all, he had pretty big sandals to fill. Could he lead the people as well as Moses had? The responsibilities must have felt overwhelming. God stepped in with encouragement and a remedy for insecurity: "Stay close to Me, read My Word, be courageous, and remember that I am with you." That's what He says to you as well.

This Is Promising
Those who fear the LORD are secure. - Proverbs 14:26

Q

What can I do with my worries?

God's Response

Give all your worries and cares to God, for He cares about you. - 1 Peter 5:7

Think about the things of heaven, not the things of earth. - Colossians 3:2

The people of Israel looked up and panicked when they saw the Egyptians overtaking them. They cried out to the Lord.... But Moses told the people, "Don't be afraid. Just stand still and watch the Lord rescue you."
- Exodus 14:10, 13

· · · ——————— · · ·

The first step in dealing with worry is to release it to the Lord in prayer. Hand it off for Him to carry. The second step is to fix your thoughts on God's power, not on the problems of life. Turn your attention away from negative, unbelieving thoughts to positive, constructive thoughts. The third step is to remind yourself of God's faithfulness to you in the past. He is still in control of the world and can still handle your problems. Combat worry by remembering and trusting God's promises and then move forward.

This Is Promising

Don't worry about anything; instead, pray about everything. Tell God what you need, and thank Him for all He has done. - Philippians 4:6

Q

Where can I turn when I start to get overwhelmed by worry?

God's Response

That is why I tell you not to worry about everyday life—whether you have enough food and drink, or enough clothes to wear. Isn't life more than food, and your body more than clothing? Look at the birds. They don't plant or harvest or store food in barns, for your heavenly Father feeds them. And aren't you far more valuable to Him than they are? Can all your worries add a single moment to your life? - Matthew 6:25-27

Worry is a natural part of life, but too much worry can distract and paralyze you, and can even lead to a sinful denial of God's presence and grace in your life. Worry crowds out what is good in your life and focuses you on your problems, which makes them seem much worse. Worry over the concerns of life becomes sinful when it prevents you from thinking about anything else, including God. The Bible teaches that we find rest from worry when we admit that we can't control the future and then entrust ourselves—and our loved ones—to the God Who does.

This Is Promising

These things dominate the thoughts of unbelievers, but your heavenly Father already knows all your needs. Seek the Kingdom of God above all else, and live righteously, and He will give you everything you need. So don't worry about tomorrow. - Matthew 6:32-34

Q Will God help me when I'm overwhelmed?

God's Response

Her sister, Mary, sat at the Lord's feet, listening to what He taught. But Martha was distracted by the big dinner she was preparing. She came to Jesus and said, "Lord, doesn't it seem unfair to You that my sister just sits here while I do all the work? Tell her to come and help me." But the Lord said to her, "My dear Martha, you are worried and upset over all these details! There is only one thing worth being concerned about. Mary has discovered it, and it will not be taken away from her." - Luke 10:39-42

Mary and Martha both loved Jesus. On this occasion, they were both serving Him, but Martha was trying so hard to serve that she was neglecting her guest and getting weighed down by His visit. Worry overwhelms the mind; God's Word relaxes the mind and puts it at peace by telling us how to overcome worry. The next time you feel beleaguered, maybe you need to sit at Jesus' feet and listen to Him.

This Is Promising

I am leaving you with a gift—peace of mind and heart.... So don't be troubled or afraid. - John 14:27

Q How I do go about making plans for the year ahead?

God's Response

David [said,] … "It was my desire to build a temple…. I made the necessary preparations for building it, but God said to me, 'You must not build a temple.'" - 1 Chronicles 28:2-3

David gave Solomon the plans for the Temple. - 1 Chronicles 28:11

"Every part of this plan," David told Solomon, "was given to me in writing from the hand of the LORD." - 1 Chronicles 28:19

I know, my God, that You examine our hearts and rejoice when You find integrity there. - 1 Chronicles 29:17

· · · ———— · · ·

It is interesting that God didn't want David to build the Temple, just to plan it and gather the materials. You may not be planning a magnificent building, but the work God has for you is just as important. Like David, make sure your plans are in tune with God's intentions for you. When making your plans, don't forget what is most important—stay close to God through Bible study, prayer, fellowship with other believers, and service. Do what is right and take responsibility for your sins. When you do these things first, God's more detailed plan for you will become clearer.

This Is Promising

Trust in the LORD with all your heart; do not depend on your own understanding. Seek His will in all you do, and He will show you which path to take. - Proverbs 3:5-6

Q How do I set priorities?

God's Response

This is what the LORD of Heaven's Armies says: Look at what's happening to you! Now go up into the hills, bring down timber, and rebuild My house. Then I will take pleasure in it and be honored, says the LORD. You hoped for rich harvests, but they were poor. And when you brought your harvest home, I blew it away. Why? Because My house lies in ruins, says the LORD of Heaven's Armies, while all of you are busy building your own fine houses.
- Haggai 1:7-9

Sometimes problems in your life just happen; they're not your fault. But the Bible is absolutely clear that sometimes your problems are your fault and have come because you've got your priorities wrong. Over and over God says that He wants what is best for you. He wants to pour His blessings on you—not always with material things, but with joy, peace, fulfillment, satisfaction, and the ability to have a big impact for His Kingdom. He won't reward you if you neglect Him, as the nation of Judah did. When you put God first, He rewards your loyalty to Him in ways you never dreamed possible. Keep God at the top of your list and you will experience much more of God's blessing.

This Is Promising
Seek the Kingdom of God above all else, and live righteously, and He will give you everything you need. - Matthew 6:33

Q How can I make God my highest priority?

God's Response

*Now, Israel, what does the L*ORD *your God require of you? He requires only that you fear the L*ORD *your God, and live in a way that pleases Him, and love Him and serve Him with all your heart and soul. And you must always obey the L*ORD*'s commands and decrees that I am giving you today for your own good. - Deuteronomy 10:12-13*

*As for me and my family, we will serve the L*ORD*. - Joshua 24:15*

Wherever your treasure is, there the desires of your heart will also be.
- Luke 12:34

. . . ——— . . .

If God is the center of your life, you will make your relationship with Him your highest priority. You will spend time in prayer and Bible reading, your thoughts will turn increasingly to God, you will begin wanting to please Him, and you will want to obey God's Word more. When you are doing these things, you are keeping God as your highest priority. You can tell how you are progressing by noticing how you spend your time each day.

This Is Promising

You must not have any other god but Me. - Exodus 20:3

Q How can I keep my life balanced?

God's Response

For everything there is a season, a time for every activity under heaven.
- Ecclesiastes 3:1

You have six days each week for your ordinary work, but on the seventh day you must stop working, even during the seasons of plowing and harvest. - Exodus 34:21

Seek the Kingdom of God above all else, and live righteously, and He will give you everything you need. - Matthew 6:33

Three things can help you balance your life. First, make spending daily time with God your top priority. Only when you put God first will you understand how to use the rest of your time. Second, keep track of how you spend your time for a week. This will quickly show what takes up most of your day. If one activity begins to dominate your time, it may be out of control and you will feel overwhelmed. Finally, understand that you may have to say "no" to some things so you can focus on accomplishing the more important things. Even Jesus had to leave some things undone so He could complete what God wanted Him to do.

This Is Promising

Simon and the others went out to find [Jesus]. When they found Him, they said, "Everyone is looking for You." But Jesus replied, "We must go on to other towns as well, and I will preach to them, too. That is why I came."
- Mark 1:36-38

Q

What causes me to become unbalanced?

God's Response

Jealousy and selfishness are not God's kind of wisdom. Such things are earthly, unspiritual, and demonic. For wherever there is jealousy and selfish ambition, there you will find disorder and evil of every kind. - James 3:15-16

Don't love money; be satisfied with what you have. For God has said, "I will never fail you. I will never abandon you." - Hebrews 13:5

Too much sleep clothes them in rags. - Proverbs 23:21

· · · ——————— · · ·

Excess in any area (too much or too little food, too much or too little sleep) leads to imbalance. Too much of anything means that there is not enough of something else—and that something else is usually God. An unbalanced lifestyle will always lead to frustration and to feeling out of control. To get your life in balance, begin with God. Ask Him to help you prioritize your activities so you have healthy amounts of food, sleep, work, play, exercise, service, and reflection.

This Is Promising

You see me when I travel and when I rest at home. You know everything I do. - Psalm 139:3

Q

Do I have the kinds of values that God desires?

God's Response

A good person produces good things from the treasury of a good heart, and an evil person produces evil things from the treasury of an evil heart. What you say flows from what is in your heart. - Luke 6:45

The LORD has told you what is good, and this is what He requires of you: to do what is right, to love mercy, and to walk humbly with your God.
- Micah 6:8

It's easy to see what you really value by the choices you make. Just consider how you spend your money and your time, what you think about most, and what gets you jazzed. Then ask yourself how you view acts that the Bible calls sin, such as lying, ignoring wrongdoing, gossip, flattery, profanity, and cheating. If you don't see these as sin, you must face the fact that your values differ from the Bible's, and your choices will not be pleasing to God.

This Is Promising

Do to others whatever you would like them to do to you. This is the essence of all that is taught in the law and the prophets. - Matthew 7:12

Q

Can I live like a Christian at school without looking weird?

God's Response

It is God's will that your honorable lives should silence those ignorant people who make foolish accusations against you. - 1 Peter 2:15

Moses told his father-in-law everything the LORD had done to Pharaoh and Egypt on behalf of Israel. He also told about all the hardships they had experienced along the way and how the LORD had rescued His people from all their troubles. Jethro was delighted when he heard about all the good things the LORD had done for Israel as He rescued them from the hand of the Egyptians. - Exodus 18:8-9

Moses told Jethro in conversation all that God had done. You can speak when it seems natural, but even more important is how you live. If your life reflects Jesus in you, many will be drawn to you. They will want to know what makes you different, and that's your opportunity to tell them. But some of your classmates will definitely think you are weird. There are always some who will mock and even hate anyone who stands up for what is right and good. It happened to Jesus, and He warned that it will happen to you. Don't let the people who love sin and evil influence you to live less like a Christian.

This Is Promising

We are Christ's ambassadors; God is making His appeal through us.
- 2 Corinthians 5:20

Q Will God help me witness about my faith?

God's Response

Come, follow me, and I will show you how to fish for people! - Mark 1:17

… when the Holy Spirit comes upon you. And you will be My witnesses, telling people about Me everywhere—in Jerusalem, throughout Judea, in Samaria, and to the ends of the earth. - Acts 1:8

One night the Lord spoke to Paul in a vision and told him, "Don't be afraid! Speak out! Don't be silent! For I am with you." - Acts 18:9-10

Telling others about faith in Jesus is easier for some than others, but Jesus wants us all to do it. As you pray for sensitivity to His leading, Jesus promises to put in front of you those He has made ready to hear the good news of salvation. You are not alone when you witness. The Holy Spirit is with you to give you the words, the strength, and the power to proclaim His message and tell your story.

This Is Promising

Has the LORD redeemed you? Then speak out! Tell others He has redeemed you from your enemies. - Psalm 107:2

Q

How do I overcome my fear of witnessing?

God's Response

Our purpose is to please God, not people. He alone examines the motives of our hearts. - 1 Thessalonians 2:4

My message and my preaching were very plain.... I relied only on the power of the Holy Spirit. - 1 Corinthians 2:4

When we brought you the Good News ... the Holy Spirit gave you full assurance that what we said was true. - 1 Thessalonians 1:5

· · · ———— · · ·

You can overcome your fear if you train yourself to be less worried about what people think of you and more concerned about their needs today and their souls in the future. Sharing your faith is literally a life-and-death decision. You are not responsible to make people believe—your job is just to share your story and the good news of salvation. The Holy Spirit will do the work in people's hearts and minds.

This Is Promising
Do not tremble; do not be afraid. Did I not proclaim My purposes for you long ago? You are My witnesses—is there any other God? No! There is no other Rock—not one! - Isaiah 44:8

Q   What should I say when I witness?

God's Response

Andrew, Simon Peter's brother, was one of these men who heard what John said and then followed Jesus. Andrew went to find his brother, Simon, and told him, "We have found the Messiah" (which means "Christ"). Then Andrew brought Simon to meet Jesus. - John 1:40-42

Many Samaritans from the village believed in Jesus because the woman had said, "He told me everything I ever did!" When they came out to see Him, they begged Him to stay in their village. So He stayed for two days, long enough for many more to hear His message and believe. - John 4:39-41

The best kind of witnessing you can do is simply to tell your story. Tell how you came to believe and what God has done in your life. Explain the hope that you have. Then invite people to investigate the truth for themselves. People can argue about theology, but they can't refute your experiences of God.

This Is Promising

Instead, you must worship Christ as Lord of your life. And if someone asks about your Christian hope, always be ready to explain it. - 1 Peter 3:15

Q

What do I do when people don't want to listen to my faith story?

God's Response

He said, "Son of man, go to the people of Israel and give them My messages. I am not sending you to a foreign people whose language you cannot understand. No, I am not sending you to people with strange and difficult speech. If I did, they would listen! But the people of Israel won't listen to you any more than they listen to Me!" - Ezekiel 3:4-7

A farmer went out to plant his seed.... Some seed fell on a footpath, where it was stepped on.... Other seed fell on fertile soil. - Luke 8:5, 8

I planted the seed in your hearts, and Apollos watered it, but it was God Who made it grow. - 1 Corinthians 3:6

· · · ——— · · ·

Ezekiel was sent to tell people about God. God already knew the people were not going to listen to Ezekiel, but he was to tell them anyway. You may share your story only to find people refusing to listen. However, you don't know if you have planted a seed in someone's heart that will one day grow into faith in Jesus.

This Is Promising

Still other seed fell on fertile soil. This seed grew and produced a crop that was a hundred times as much as had been planted! - Luke 8:8

Q Some of my teachers make fun of my faith. How should I respond to them—or should I?

God's Response

When they heard Paul speak about the resurrection of the dead, some laughed in contempt, but others said, "We want to hear more about this later." That ended Paul's discussion with them, but some joined him and became believers. - Acts 17:32-34

If you face teachers who make fun of your faith, pray about how to respond to them. You should always be respectful, just as Paul was. It will take courage and strength to face opposition or even derision, but your job is to share your faith and allow God to work in their hearts. Some may laugh, but you don't know how other teachers or students will be affected by your consistent witness and godly lifestyle. One thing is for sure: God will be pleased and you will be blessed.

This Is Promising

Those who are wise will shine as bright as the sky, and those who lead many to righteousness will shine like the stars forever. - Daniel 12:3

Q Sometimes I hear people accusing Christians of being hypocrites. How can I avoid being a hypocrite?

God's Response

Hypocrite! First get rid of the log in your own eye; then you will see well enough to deal with the speck in your friend's eye. - Matthew 7:5

Hypocrites! For you are so careful to clean the outside of the cup and the dish, but inside you are filthy—full of greed and self-indulgence!
- Matthew 23:25

Hypocrites! For you are like whitewashed tombs—beautiful on the outside but filled on the inside with dead people's bones and all sorts of impurity.
- Matthew 23:27

· · · ———— · · ·

Jesus called many religious people hypocrites because they knew the Scriptures but did not live by them. Today, as in Jesus' day, many people who know the Bible do not let it change their lives. They say they follow Jesus, but they don't live by His standards of love and obedience. They go to church, but not for the right reasons. People who say one thing and live something different are hypocrites. You can avoid being a hypocrite by making sure that your actions match what you say you believe.

This Is Promising
False prophets and those who seek their guidance will all be punished for their sins. - Ezekiel 14:10

September

Q

How can I be my own person without being rebellious against my parents or against God?

God's Response

The Holy Spirit says, "Today when you hear His voice, don't harden your hearts as Israel did when they rebelled, when they tested Me in the wilderness. There your ancestors tested and tried My patience, even though they saw My miracles for forty years. So I was angry with them, and I said, 'Their hearts always turn away from Me. They refuse to do what I tell them.'" - Hebrews 3:7-10

At this time in life, you're tired of being told what to do; you want to chart your own course and become your own person. Great! Go for it! But being your own person and being rebellious are two totally different things. Authority is not always a bad thing—the abuse of authority is a bad thing. God's authority will not only save your life but will show you how to be successful and blessed. Don't rebel against that authority and jeopardize your very soul. Being your own person doesn't mean doing whatever you want to; it means using your God-given personality and talents to serve Him through serving others.

This Is Promising

Be careful then, dear brothers and sisters. Make sure that your own hearts are not evil and unbelieving, turning you away from the living God.
- Hebrews 3:12

Q Is rebellion ever good?

God's Response

You have had enough in the past of the evil things that godless people enjoy—their immorality and lust, their feasting and drunkenness and wild parties, and their terrible worship of idols. Of course, your former friends are surprised when you no longer plunge into the flood of wild and destructive things they do. So they slander you. But remember that they will have to face God, Who will judge everyone, both the living and the dead. - 1 Peter 4:3-5

When under pressure to participate in sinful activities, you as a Christian must rebel against the crowd. Sure, you may find yourself being made fun of because you refuse to participate in certain activities. Your priorities have changed and you are now heading in the opposite direction, so you have to rebel against actions that would displease God. Be a rebel with a cause—of obedience, purity, and love for God.

This Is Promising

But if you rebel against the LORD's commands and refuse to listen to Him, then His hand will be as heavy upon you as it was upon your ancestors.
- 1 Samuel 12:15

Q Does God want me to be different from the world around me?

God's Response

But Daniel was determined not to defile himself by eating the food and wine given to them by the king. He asked the chief of staff for permission not to eat these unacceptable foods.... "Please test us for ten days on a diet of vegetables and water." ... At the end of the ten days, Daniel and his three friends looked healthier and better nourished than the young men who had been eating the food assigned by the king. - Daniel 1:8, 12, 15

Daniel was able to be a nonconformist and live faithfully in an environment opposed to his faith. He won respect by his wise living, his wise ways of dealing with those around him, and his hard work. His obedience in this situation prepared him for the tough tests of obedience to come. You don't have to be a weirdo; stick to your principles while living with kindness, respect, and hard work.

This Is Promising

What counts is whether we have been transformed into a new creation.
- Galatians 6:15

Q

How can I let God know that
I'm available for Him to use?

God's Response

*One of the seraphim flew to me with a burning coal he had taken from
the altar with a pair of tongs. He touched my lips with it and said, "See,
this coal has touched your lips. Now your guilt is removed, and your sins
are forgiven." Then I heard the Lord asking, "Whom should I send as a
messenger to this people? Who will go for Us?" I said, "Here I am. Send
me." - Isaiah 6:6-8*

If you want God to know that you're available, tell Him so. God may
have to make some preparations in your heart and life—as He had
to cleanse Isaiah's lips before Isaiah could speak for Him. Letting
God prepare you may be difficult or even painful, but you will be
ready to represent Him. That's a job you don't want to turn down!

This Is Promising

*If you keep yourself pure, you will be a special utensil for honorable use.
Your life will be clean, and you will be ready for the Master to use you for
every good work. - 2 Timothy 2:21*

Q How does God expect me to behave?

God's Response

You received God's Spirit when He adopted you as His own children. Now we call Him, "Abba, Father." - Romans 8:15

Don't copy the behavior and customs of this world, but let God transform you into a new person by changing the way you think. - Romans 12:2

Get rid of all evil behavior. Be done with all deceit, hypocrisy, jealousy, and all unkind speech. - 1 Peter 2:1

Actions speak louder than words. Your behavior is eloquent testimony to who you are and what you believe. The Bible calls you to godly living, and if you have been transformed by Jesus Christ, then His Holy Spirit is living within you, helping you want to do what is right. Godly living confirms that you are, in fact, living for God and not just yourself. This barometer of your relationship with Him means that you are trying your best to be like Jesus.

This Is Promising

For once you were full of darkness, but now you have light from the Lord. So live as people of light! - Ephesians 5:8

Q Does my behavior affect others?

God's Response

Let your good deeds shine out for all to see, so that everyone will praise your heavenly Father. - Matthew 5:16

Because we belong to the day, we must live decent lives for all to see.
- Romans 13:13

Your godly lives will speak to them without any words. They will be won over by observing your pure and reverent lives. - 1 Peter 3:1-2

Godly living is an example to unbelieving friends, neighbors, and coworkers. Sometimes your godly life speaks better than any words. When people see how you live and speak, they will want to know what makes you different. You then have a wonderful opportunity to tell them. Saint Francis of Assisi once said, "Preach the gospel at all times; if necessary, use words."

This Is Promising

Oh, that my actions would consistently reflect Your decrees! - Psalm 119:5

Q

What are the signs of godly behavior?

God's Response

Light shines in the darkness for the godly. They are generous, compassionate, and righteous. - Psalm 112:4

The godly will rejoice in the LORD and find shelter in Him. And those who do what is right will praise Him. - Psalm 64:10

Let the godly rejoice. Let them be glad in God's presence. Let them be filled with joy. - Psalm 68:3

· · · ——— · ·

Godly people want to be as much like God as possible. Godly people will be loving, kind, helpful, and generous with their time and money. Their language will be clean, their thoughts and actions will be pure, and they will be joyful. They learn to be like this by reading God's Word, meditating on God's character, and deciding to please God with their lives.

This Is Promising

Since everything around us is going to be destroyed like this, what holy and godly lives you should live. - 2 Peter 3:11

Q How should I honor and respect my parents?

God's Response

Each of you must show great respect for your mother and father.
- *Leviticus 19:3*

You let them disregard their needy parents. And so you cancel the word of God in order to hand down your own tradition. - *Mark 7:12-13*

Children, obey your parents because you belong to the Lord, for this is the right thing to do. - *Ephesians 6:1*

. . . ———— . . .

Why is God so strict about honoring parents? First, honoring others acknowledges the value God places on all people, regardless of how righteous or sinful they are. Second, your parents are the ones who gave you life, the most precious gift God gives us after salvation. Third, a parent/child relationship represents God's parent/child relationship with us, His children. As we honor our parents, we demonstrate our respect and love for God. Even if you have abusive or neglectful parents, you can still honor them by acknowledging that they are created by God, and that they gave you the gift of life.

This Is Promising

If you honor your father and mother, "things will go well for you, and you will have a long life on the earth." - *Ephesians 6:3*

Q

What if the leaders of my country leave something to be desired? How do I respond?

God's Response

Everyone must submit to governing authorities. For all authority comes from God, and those in positions of authority have been placed there by God. So anyone who rebels against authority is rebelling against what God has instituted, and they will be punished. - Romans 13:1-2

We must obey God rather than any human authority. - Acts 5:29

We should be responsible citizens as well as responsible Christians. Every government is in power because God allows it to be. Therefore, you should work hard to obey the laws of your land and make your country better. The Bible is also clear that you should never violate God's moral standards. This means that you should never allow the government to force you to disobey God. You should not disobey the government for personal reasons, but only for moral reasons when God's laws are violated. Civil disobedience comes with a price, so if you are compelled to disobey, you must be courageous enough to accept the consequences and defend your faith in the Lord.

This Is Promising

If you look carefully into the perfect law that sets you free, and if you do what it says and don't forget what you heard, then God will bless you for doing it. - James 1:25

Q

Can I have qualities that will make others look up to me?

God's Response

Whoever wants to be a leader among you must be your servant.
- Matthew 20:26

I pressed further, "What you are doing is not right!" - Nehemiah 5:9

He must become greater and greater, and I must become less and less.
- John 3:30

If you want to be looked up to by your peers, then have a servant's heart, take responsibility for your actions (don't pass the buck when it's convenient), refuse to stay silent when things are wrong, and do not seek glory for yourself. The world has taught you to look and act cool, to use coarse or foul language, to disrespect authority, and to bend the rules as far as you can. In the end, it will be the people who have consistently lived with kindness, integrity, and a deep love for God Who will be most respected and honored.

This Is Promising

I will give you shepherds after my own heart, who will guide you with knowledge and understanding. - Jeremiah 3:15

Q

September 11 is a day to remember heroes.
What types of people should be my heroes?

God's Response

The godly people in the land are my true heroes! - Psalm 16:3

All these people earned a good reputation because of their faith, yet none of them received all that God had promised. For God had something better in mind for us, so that they would not reach perfection without us.
- Hebrews 11:39-40

God's heroes are those who hang on to their faith in Him no matter what happens. The Bible is full of examples of people who never stopped trusting God even though they were mocked, persecuted, and killed for their faith. God may not ask you to be a martyr for Him, but is your faith strong enough to endure even a little derision or scorn? Those who live boldly for God despite opposition will make the greatest impact for eternity.

This Is Promising

We give great honor to those who endure under suffering. For instance, you know about Job, a man of great endurance. You can see how the Lord was kind to him at the end, for the Lord is full of tenderness and mercy.
- James 5:11

What are some bad habits that I should avoid?

God's Response

Pharaoh again became stubborn and refused to let the people go.
- Exodus 8:32

Soon the people began to complain about their hardship, and the LORD heard everything they said. Then the LORD's anger blazed against them.
- Numbers 11:1

They will learn to be lazy and will spend their time gossiping.
- 1 Timothy 5:13

The habit of intentionally disobeying God's Word can eventually lead to a hard heart that can no longer be touched by God's Spirit. When you harden your heart against God, He may eventually let you get locked into your stubborn pride and unbelief. As a believer, it is essential to keep your heart soft so that you can listen to God and obey His words. It is a frightening judgment when God allows a person to remain in their sin. God's grace alone opens people's eyes and makes them ready to believe.

This Is Promising

Make sure that your own hearts are not evil and unbelieving, turning you away from the living God. You must warn each other every day, while it is still "today," so that none of you will be deceived by sin and hardened against God. For if we are faithful to the end, trusting God just as firmly as when we first believed, we will share in all that belongs to Christ. - Hebrews 3:12-14

Q

Can God help me get rid of bad habits and develop good habits?

God's Response

Don't you realize that you become the slave of whatever you choose to obey? You can be a slave to sin, which leads to death, or you can choose to obey God, which leads to righteous living. - Romans 6:16

Train yourself to be godly. Physical training is good, but training for godliness is much better, promising benefits in this life and in the life to come. - 1 Timothy 4:7-8

Just as it takes time to kick a bad habit, so it takes time to develop a good habit. God will help you do both, but be patient. You get rid of bad habits by asking for God's help, and you're also going to need some good old-fashioned discipline and self-control. Good habits—such as reading God's Word, praying, and giving your time and money in service—will be developed as you do them. The more you do them, the more natural they will become.

This Is Promising

All athletes are disciplined in their training. They do it to win a prize that will fade away, but we do it for an eternal prize. - 1 Corinthians 9:25

Q

Of what benefit are the rules God sets in the Bible?

God's Response

The LORD God warned him, "You may freely eat the fruit of every tree in the garden—except the tree of the knowledge of good and evil. If you eat its fruit, you are sure to die." - Genesis 2:16-17

Obey the LORD's commands and decrees that I am giving you today for your own good. - Deuteronomy 10:13

When you were little, your parents may have had a rule about not playing in the street. The rule was not made to wreck your fun, but to keep you safe and alive so you could have more fun for a longer period of time! The rule was made out of love. The same is true of God's rules. He makes them so your life can be safer, more enjoyable, and more fulfilling. After all, He created life, so He knows how you can get the most out of it. So start reading God's rule book, the Bible, and enjoy life to its fullest.

This Is Promising

See how I love Your commandments, LORD. - Psalm 119:159

Q Can I be a good leader?

God's Response

King Rehoboam discussed the matter with the older men who had counseled his father, Solomon. "What is your advice?" he asked. "How should I answer these people?" The older counselors replied, "If you are willing to be a servant to these people today and give them a favorable answer, they will always be your loyal subjects." But Rehoboam rejected the advice of the older men and instead asked the opinion of the young men who had grown up with him and were now his advisers. - 1 Kings 12:6-8

The mark of a good leader is that you are a good listener, and that you listen to the right people. King Rehoboam had inherited a mighty kingdom from his father; but he destroyed it by listening to the wrong people and following their advice. As you move forward in life, you will certainly find yourself in some kind of leadership role. Seek out godly people who are older and wiser than you, who want to serve others and don't care about personal gain. Ask God for advice as well. Then you know you will be doing the right things.

This Is Promising
Fools think their own way is right, but the wise listen to others.
- Proverbs 12:15

Q Can I learn from Jesus about being a good leader?

God's Response

The Son can do nothing by Himself. He does only what He sees the Father doing. Whatever the Father does, the Son also does. - John 5:19

Jesus called His twelve disciples together and gave them authority to cast out evil spirits and to heal every kind of disease and illness. - Matthew 10:1

Since I, your Lord and Teacher, have washed your feet, you ought to wash each other's feet. - John 13:14

Part of a leader's responsibility is to help his or her followers develop a perspective on God's truth that enables them to interpret life from an eternal point of view. Even when it is hard, the truth sets people free from ignorance and deception. As a leader, it is your responsibility to keep God's truth at the center of all you do and decide. Then you will be doing what is wise and approved of by God. This applies whether you are the leader of a family, a church group, or a large corporation.

This Is Promising

I have given you an example to follow. Do as I have done to you. - John 13:15

Q Some of my friends are lazy and never do homework or school activities. Occasionally I'd like to join them. What's so bad about that?

God's Response

Lazy people are soon poor; hard workers get rich. - Proverbs 10:4

Lazy people want much but get little, but those who work hard will prosper. - Proverbs 13:4

Never be lazy, but work hard and serve the Lord enthusiastically.
- Romans 12:11

There is a difference between rest and laziness. The Bible clearly says that laziness is a sin, while rest is a reward for hard work. Someday you will be asked to give an account for how you spent your time on earth. Your responsibility now is to work hard and do well in school, which is presently your full-time job. When you've finished your work and done a good job, reward yourself with some needed rest. The day will come when you will have to provide for yourself. Don't get into the habit of laziness—it will hurt you for the rest of your life.

This Is Promising

Work hard and become a leader; be lazy and become a slave. - Proverbs 12:24

Q Can God give me a better attitude toward school?

God's Response

"Why have you brought us out of Egypt to die here in the wilderness?" they complained. "There is nothing to eat here and nothing to drink. And we hate this horrible manna!" - Numbers 21:5

Always be full of joy in the Lord. I say it again—rejoice! ... Don't worry about anything; instead, pray about everything. Tell God what you need, and thank Him for all He has done. - Philippians 4:4-6

This is the day the LORD has made. We will rejoice and be glad in it. - Psalm 118:24

Your outlook on life determines how you view your challenges. School is a challenge. If you see it only as a bother, you will develop an attitude of bitterness, cynicism, and carelessness that will make every day seem like a burden. If you see it as an opportunity for strengthening your character, building your future, and testing your godly convictions, then you will be able to rise above the challenges and develop a better attitude toward school. Right now God has put you here for a reason. Don't squander the opportunities God has given you.

This Is Promising

A cheerful heart is good medicine. - Proverbs 17:22

Q I'm just not motivated to do well in school. How can God help?

God's Response

But on the judgment day, fire will reveal what kind of work each builder has done. The fire will show if a person's work has any value. If the work survives, that builder will receive a reward. But if the work is burned up, the builder will suffer great loss. The builder will be saved, but like someone barely escaping through a wall of flames. - 1 Corinthians 3:13-15

As a follower of Christ, you are already saved, but there will one day be an evaluation of your work. God isn't worried about how good your grades are, but He does want to know that you did your best, made the most of your time, and used the opportunities He gave you. Your opportunity now is to learn and to mature in your faith. Make the most of it.

This Is Promising

Our goal is to please Him.... We will each receive whatever we deserve.
- 2 Corinthians 5:9-10

Q My school activities leave me no time for church stuff. Is it okay to be more dedicated right now to my school activities than to youth group?

God's Response

The church is His body; it is made full and complete by Christ, Who fills all things everywhere with Himself. - Ephesians 1:23

The human body has many parts, but the many parts make up one whole body. So it is with the body of Christ. - 1 Corinthians 12:12

Although sports and other interests are important, you need to set priorities so that you can attend church and be a part of a small group. If you must miss church for a time, get back to it as soon as possible so that you don't get out of the habit of attending. As a believer, you are part of God's family. Only by meeting together can you stay connected to that family, which is essential for growing in your faith, being accountable for your actions, and giving and receiving encouragement to stay loyal to God. The church needs you because the body of Christ is not complete unless you are there!

This Is Promising

Let us not neglect our meeting together, as some people do, but encourage one another. - Hebrews 10:25

Q

Everyone I know cheats—some more than others—in order to get decent grades. Why is it so important to be honest?

God's Response

Do not deceive or cheat one another. - Leviticus 19:11

What shall I say about the homes of the wicked filled with treasures gained by cheating? What about the disgusting practice of measuring out grain with dishonest measures? - Micah 6:10

Better to have little, with godliness, than to be rich and dishonest.
- Proverbs 16:8

Honesty creates trust, and trust is the basis of all relationships. If you can't trust someone, you won't want to be a close friend. If people can't trust you, they won't ask you to be their friend. God wants you to be completely honest in your life because that is the only way to have a good reputation and be a good example of Christian living. When you are honest in all details, you experience the distinct advantages of having a clear conscience, earning the trust and respect of others, as well as God's blessing. You can build a good reputation by consistent, honest behavior, and you can start today.

This Is Promising

The LORD detests the use of dishonest scales, but He delights in accurate weights. - Proverbs 11:1

Why does cheating, on a large or small scale, matter to God?

God's Response

All who cheat with dishonest weights and measures are detestable to the LORD your God. - Deuteronomy 25:16

The LORD detests double standards; He is not pleased by dishonest scales. - Proverbs 20:23

The LORD demands accurate scales and balances; He sets the standards for fairness. - Proverbs 16:11

If you are faithful in little things, you will be faithful in large ones. But if you are dishonest in little things, you won't be honest with greater responsibilities. - Luke 16:10

People who want God's blessing must abide by God's standards of fairness and justice. God is so concerned about cheating that He even made laws about the scales for weighing grain in the marketplace. Cheating matters greatly to God because it reveals a severe character flaw. If you have developed the habit of cheating, it will be very difficult to stop when bigger challenges with bigger stakes come your way. If you can't be trusted to be honest in a small matter, you can't be trusted to be honest in a big matter.

This Is Promising

Love does no wrong to others, so love fulfills the requirements of God's law. - Romans 13:10

Q

Does character really matter? Is it overrated?

God's Response

Suppose a certain man is righteous and does what is just and right.... He is a merciful creditor ... He does not rob the poor but instead gives food to the hungry and provides clothes for the needy. He ... stays away from injustice, is honest and fair when judging others, and faithfully obeys My decrees and regulations. Anyone who does these things is just and will surely live, says the Sovereign LORD. - Ezekiel 18:5, 7-9

Even children are known by the way they act, whether their conduct is pure, and whether it is right. - Proverbs 20:11

If you perform well on the job or in school, do the actions of your personal life really matter? Yes. Justice, righteousness, integrity, mercy, honesty, fairness, and faithfulness are essential traits of a godly person's character because they reflect who a person really is. For example, you cannot be honest in your job and be a liar and a cheat in your personal life. It doesn't work that way. You are who you are, twenty-four hours a day. If you demonstrate ungodly characteristics, you can be sure that they will surface in all areas of your life—personal and public.

This Is Promising

If you are faithful in little things, you will be faithful in large ones. But if you are dishonest in little things, you won't be honest with greater responsibilities. - Luke 16:10

Q Are there consequences for being dishonest? I see people every day who seem to get away with it.

God's Response

There was a certain man named Ananias who, with his wife, Sapphira, sold some property. He brought part of the money to the apostles, claiming it was the full amount. With his wife's consent, he kept the rest. Then Peter said, "Ananias, why have you let Satan fill your heart? … You weren't lying to us but to God!" As soon as Ananias heard these words, he fell to the floor and died. - Acts 5:1-5

The sin Ananias and Sapphira committed was lying to God and God's people—trying to make themselves appear more generous than they really were. This act was judged severely because dishonesty, greed, and coveting what others have are so destructive to honest relationships. All lying is bad, but when people lie to God and other believers, they destroy their testimony. Your friends may not be getting caught now, but a habit of dishonesty will follow them throughout life and will eventually catch up with them.

This Is Promising

Dishonesty destroys treacherous people. - Proverbs 11:3

Q

Does God care about my motives as long as I do the right thing?

God's Response

I know, my God, that You examine our hearts and rejoice when You find integrity there. You know I have done all this with good motives.
- 1 Chronicles 29:17

The sacrifice of an evil person is detestable, especially when it is offered with wrong motives. - Proverbs 21:27

When you give to someone in need, don't let your left hand know what your right hand is doing. Give your gifts in private, and your Father, who sees everything, will reward you. - Matthew 6:3-4

· · · · · · ·

God is as interested in your motives as in your behavior, for eventually, selfish and sinful motives produce selfish and sinful behavior. People can find an excuse for doing almost anything, but God looks behind the excuses to the motives of the heart. Check your motives by asking, "Would God be pleased with my real reasons for doing this?" and "Would I still be willing to do this if I knew everyone would find out?"

This Is Promising

The LORD's light penetrates the human spirit, exposing every hidden motive. - Proverbs 20:27

Q What are some wrong motives?

God's Response

Why did [Cain] kill [Abel]? Because Cain had been doing what was evil, and his brother had been doing what was righteous. - 1 John 3:12

Their mouths are full of lustful words, and their hearts seek only after money. - Ezekiel 33:31

Watch out! Don't do your good deeds publicly, to be admired by others. - Matthew 6:1

When Simon saw that the Spirit was given when the apostles laid their hands on people, he offered them money to buy this power. "Let me have this power, too," he exclaimed, "so that when I lay my hands on people, they will receive the Holy Spirit!" - Acts 8:18-19

Your motives matter to God because they expose whether you're working for God or for yourself. When your motives are selfish or impure, it's only a matter of time before your actions are also selfish and impure. God is far more concerned about the condition of your heart than He is with your external behavior, because He knows that your behavior flows from your heart. Remember that God alone knows your heart. You may be able to fool others and yourself, but you can't fool God.

This Is Promising

If you plan to do evil, you will be lost; if you plan to do good, you will receive unfailing love and faithfulness. - Proverbs 14:22

Q

What are pure motives?

God's Response

May the words of my mouth and the meditation of my heart be pleasing to You, O LORD. - Psalm 19:14

Put me on trial, LORD, and cross-examine me. Test my motives and my heart. - Psalm 26:2

He will bring our darkest secrets to light and will reveal our private motives. Then God will give to each one whatever praise is due.
- 1 Corinthians 4:5

. . . —————— . . .

God desires a teachable heart that has integrity and is pure, joyful, and devoted. This kind of heart honors and delights Him. We will never fully achieve these qualities in this life, but God is pleased when we truly desire a heart like this. Do your best to move in that direction today.

This Is Promising

Fire tests the purity of silver and gold, but the LORD tests the heart.
- Proverbs 17:3

How does my conscience work?
What is the danger of ignoring it?

God's Response

David confessed to Nathan, "I have sinned against the LORD."
- 2 Samuel 12:13

They know the truth about God because He has made it obvious to them.
- Romans 1:19

Cling to your faith in Christ, and keep your conscience clear. For some people have deliberately violated their consciences; as a result, their faith has been shipwrecked. - 1 Timothy 1:19

· · · ——— · · ·

David felt guilty when confronted with his sin. Your conscience is a gift from God, an instinct He has placed inside you that makes you aware of your sins and gives you an appropriate sense of guilt when you have done wrong. It then calls you to act by righting the wrong and receiving forgiveness from God and others. Ignoring your conscience dulls it and allows sin to grow unchecked without your feeling bad about it. This is like ignoring warning lights at a railroad crossing when a freight train is barreling down on you.

This Is Promising

Blessed are those who fear to do wrong, but the stubborn are headed for serious trouble. - Proverbs 28:14

Q
Why does it seem that some people don't even have a conscience?

God's Response

A murderer's tormented conscience will drive him into the grave. Don't protect him! - Proverbs 28:17

These people are hypocrites and liars, and their consciences are dead. - 1 Timothy 4:2

Everything is pure to those whose hearts are pure. But nothing is pure to those who are corrupt and unbelieving, because their minds and consciences are corrupted. - Titus 1:15

Everybody has a conscience, but some have become so dulled to its urgings that they don't or can't hear it. The conscience is like a muscle that must be exercised and developed. Even people who have done horrible deeds still have a conscience, but over time they have learned to tune it out. When you sin, you go against your conscience. If you don't listen to your conscience, it will eventually become calloused and insensitive to sin. Then you are in danger of not being able to hear God's voice when He warns you of danger.

This Is Promising

Keep your conscience clear. - 1 Peter 3:16

Q   Can I keep a clear conscience?

God's Response

I will maintain my innocence without wavering. My conscience is clear for as long as I live. - Job 27:6

I always try to maintain a clear conscience before God and all people. - Acts 24:16

One person believes it's all right to eat anything. But another believer with a sensitive conscience will eat only vegetables. Those who feel free to eat anything must not look down on those who don't. And those who don't eat certain foods must not condemn those who do, for God has accepted them. - Romans 14:2-3

The best way to keep a clear conscience is to steer clear of actions forbidden by Scripture. Sometimes, however, Scripture is silent, and then you should follow your conscience. When God shows you that something is wrong for you, avoid it, but don't look down on other Christians who exercise freedom in those areas.

This Is Promising

My conscience is clear, but that doesn't prove I'm right. It is the Lord Himself who will examine me and decide. - 1 Corinthians 4:4

October

Q Do my words really matter?

God's Response

If you claim to be religious but don't control your tongue, you are fooling yourself, and your religion is worthless. - James 1:26

I tell you this, you must give an account on judgment day for every idle word you speak. The words you say will either acquit you or condemn you. - Matthew 12:36-37

A gentle answer deflects anger, but harsh words make tempers flare. - Proverbs 15:1

What comes out of your mouth shows what is in your heart. Your words show what kind of person you really are. Criticism, gossip, flattery, lying, and profanity are not only "word" problems, but "heart" problems as well. Being more careful with your words isn't enough. You must first have a change of heart, and then good, kind, and healing words will follow.

This Is Promising

Wise words are more valuable than much gold and many rubies.
- Proverbs 20:15

Q What kinds of words should I speak?

God's Response

He reassured them by speaking kindly to them. - Genesis 50:21

Let everything you say be good and helpful, so that your words will be an encouragement to those who hear them. - Ephesians 4:29

Gentle words are a tree of life. - Proverbs 15:4

· · · ———— · · ·

When you open your mouth to speak, you either shoot a sharp arrow that pierces another person, inflicting hurt and pain, or you send out a soothing balm that covers a person with encouragement and healing. Sometimes you don't even realize what your words do to others. The words you say and the way that you say them can have great power and influence in others' lives. Use them wisely to bring hope and healing.

This Is Promising

May the words of my mouth and the meditation of my heart be pleasing to You, O LORD, my rock and my redeemer. - Psalm 19:14

Q Why is it so bad to swear? Everyone does it.

God's Response

You must not misuse the name of the LORD your God. - Exodus 20:7

Anyone who dishonors father or mother must be put to death.
- Exodus 21:17

*Obscene stories, foolish talk, and coarse jokes—these are not for you.
Instead, let there be thankfulness to God.* - Ephesians 5:4

· · · ———— · · ·

To profane something, whether the flag of your nation or the name of God, is to make common what ought to be respected or holy. It means to pollute that which is pure. When you use the names God or Jesus Christ as swear words, you profane Their holy names by making them common or being derogatory. When you lace your speech with coarse, vulgar language, you profane God and yourself. As a new creature in Christ, you are to be clean on the inside. Jesus taught that it's not what goes into your mouth that is sinful, but what comes out. You must be careful that your speech is pure and above reproach.

This Is Promising

Does anyone want to live a life that is long and prosperous? Then keep your tongue from speaking evil and your lips from telling lies!
- Psalm 34:12-13

Sometimes I don't feel strong enough to maintain my faith. Why does it seem so hard?

God's Response

This is what the LORD says: … "The sun will set for you prophets, and your day will come to an end. Then you seers will be put to shame, and you fortune-tellers will be disgraced. And you will cover your faces because there is no answer from God." But as for me, I am filled with power—with the Spirit of the LORD. I am filled with justice and strength to boldly declare Israel's sin and rebellion. - Micah 3:5-8

Micah faced the daunting task of preaching to people who were drifting from God and clearly rebelling against Him. Micah might not have felt strong enough for that difficult battle, but God gave Micah His Spirit so that Micah would have the discernment to know justice and truth, and have the strength to fight for them. You don't need to be strong enough to maintain your faith; you need the strength of God's Spirit working through you. Make sure that you are tapping into His power source.

This Is Promising

As for me, I look to the LORD for help. I wait confidently for God to save me, and my God will certainly hear me. - Micah 7:7

Q The Bible says that nothing is impossible for God. Some situations in my life feel impossible. Will God really help me?

God's Response

One of them said, "I will return to you about this time next year, and your wife, Sarah, will have a son!" Sarah was listening to this conversation from the tent. Abraham and Sarah were both very old by this time, and Sarah was long past the age of having children. So she laughed silently to herself and said, "How could a worn-out woman like me enjoy such pleasure, especially when my master—my husband—is also so old?" - Genesis 18:10-12

If anything seemed impossible, it was God's promise to Abraham and Sarah. He promised them a son, but many years had passed and now they were too old. Ninety-year-old women don't bear children, but God is all-powerful. He specializes in making what is impossible happen. He does this so that you know for sure that it is His power working through you, and not your own, and you learn to rely on Him more faithfully. Instead of looking at the size of the problem, look at the size of your God.

This Is Promising

The LORD said to Abraham, … "Is anything too hard for the LORD? I will return about this time next year, and Sarah will have a son."
- *Genesis 18:13-14*

Q Can God use an impossible situation to accomplish His will for me?

God's Response

The LORD said to Moses, "Has My arm lost its power? Now you will see whether or not My word comes true!" - Numbers 11:23

Even when there was no reason for hope, Abraham kept hoping—believing that he would become the father of many nations. For God had said to him, "That's how many descendants you will have!" - Romans 4:18

God can be trusted to keep His promise. - Hebrews 10:23

Too often our own limitations cause us to doubt God's ability to work through us. We make excuses for why we think things won't happen instead of thinking about how they might happen, especially when we follow an almighty God! The next time you think that a promise from God is impossible, or that you are facing an impossible problem, look at the issue again from God's perspective. Ask Him to do the impossible in you. God works most powerfully through our weaknesses.

This Is Promising

God has given both His promise and His oath. These two things are unchangeable because it is impossible for God to lie. Therefore, we who have fled to Him for refuge can have great confidence as we hold to the hope that lies before us. - Hebrews 6:18

Q

Many things are happening that distract me from my faith. How can I deal with the distractions?

God's Response

Peter called to Him, "Lord, if it's really You, tell me to come to You, walking on the water." "Yes, come," Jesus said. So Peter went over the side of the boat and walked on the water toward Jesus. But when he saw the strong wind and the waves, he was terrified and began to sink. "Save me, Lord!" he shouted. Jesus immediately reached out and grabbed him. "You have so little faith," Jesus said. "Why did you doubt Me?" - Matthew 14:28-31

Distractions take our focus off of Jesus. We can be in the middle of doing great things, but if we take our eyes off of Jesus even for a moment, we begin to sink! Distractions prevent us from moving toward God into unfamiliar territory that helps us grow and brings great rewards. You can't focus on the distractions of life and still get closer to God. Make clear goals regularly for how you will serve God, and then follow those goals without wavering. You will be less likely to be sidetracked by distractions.

This Is Promising

Remember what happened to Lot's wife! If you cling to your life, you will lose it, and if you let your life go, you will save it. - Luke 17:32-33

Q

I'm just an ordinary person—there's nothing special about me. Why would God use me?

God's Response

The members of the council were amazed when they saw the boldness of Peter and John, for they could see that they were ordinary men with no special training in the Scriptures. - Acts 4:13

Live in harmony with each other. Don't be too proud to enjoy the company of ordinary people. - Romans 12:16

This message was given to Amos, a shepherd from the town of Tekoa in Judah. - Amos 1:1

Samuel asked, "Are these all the sons you have?" "There is still the youngest," Jesse replied. "But he's out in the fields watching the sheep and goats." ... The LORD said, "This is the one; anoint him."
- 1 Samuel 16:11-12

While God sometimes uses angels and miracles, He more often chooses ordinary people doing ordinary things to accomplish something extraordinary. One day God may call you to do something extraordinary, but meanwhile, get to work serving and obeying Him. Then you'll be ready when He calls.

This Is Promising

God chose things the world considers foolish in order to shame those who think they are wise. And He chose things that are powerless to shame those who are powerful. - 1 Corinthians 1:27

Q

When does drinking become wrong?

God's Response

You have had enough … of the evil things that godless people enjoy—their immorality and lust, their feasting and drunkenness and wild parties, and their terrible worship of idols. - 1 Peter 4:3

Who has anguish? Who has sorrow? Who is always fighting? Who is always complaining? Who has unnecessary bruises? Who has bloodshot eyes? It is the one who spends long hours in the taverns, trying out new drinks. Don't gaze at the wine, seeing how red it is, how it sparkles in the cup, how smoothly it goes down. For in the end it bites like a poisonous snake; it stings like a viper. - Proverbs 23:29-32

Alcoholic beverages consumed wisely are not automatically bad. In fact, the Bible calls a good glass of wine a gift from God for our enjoyment (Psalm 104:15, John 2:1-10). But God prohibits excessive drinking. Although the Bible gives adults of legal age the freedom to drink in moderation, if your drinking causes problems for another Christian's conscience or becomes a problem for you, God asks you to abstain (Romans 14:14-16). Drinking is wrong when it leads to drunkenness, controls your actions, or causes you to disobey God. Until you are of legal age, it's always wrong. If you can't drink without dishonoring God, then you must not drink at all.

This Is Promising

Don't be drunk with wine, because that will ruin your life. Instead, be filled with the Holy Spirit. - Ephesians 5:18

Q

What does the Bible say about drugs?

God's Response

They promise freedom, but they themselves are slaves of sin and corruption. For you are a slave to whatever controls you. - 2 Peter 2:19

Don't you realize that your body is the temple of the Holy Spirit, Who lives in you and was given to you by God? You do not belong to yourself, for God bought you with a high price. So you must honor God with your body. - 1 Corinthians 6:19-20

Although the Bible doesn't talk about drugs as we know them today, it does talk about not being enslaved to anything by giving it control over your life. Experimenting with drugs leads to addiction, and whatever has control over you is your master. Addicts have given control of their lives over to a harsh master that will destroy them. To honor God, let Him be master of your life, and keep your body pure so that you can be used by Him.

This Is Promising

Whether you eat or drink, or whatever you do, do it all for the glory of God. - 1 Corinthians 10:31

Q   Can I confront someone effectively?

God's Response

They confronted King Uzziah and said, "It is not for you, Uzziah, to burn incense to the LORD. That is the work of the priests alone." - 2 Chronicles 26:18

I wrote that letter in great anguish, with a troubled heart and many tears. I didn't want to grieve you, but I wanted to let you know how much love I have for you. - 2 Corinthians 2:4

If another believer sins against you, go privately and point out the offense. If the other person listens and confesses it, you have won that person back. - Matthew 18:15

· · · ———— · · ·

Love means that you must sometimes confront someone you care about. When you need to do so, check your motives. Make sure that you are going to the person for good reasons and always go in person, as many times the problem is just a miscommunication. Do not gossip about the problem or get others involved. If you must confront, sandwich your concern between words of love and affirmation.

This Is Promising

Wounds from a sincere friend are better than many kisses from an enemy.
- Proverbs 27:6

Q

Can I resolve a conflict I have with someone?

God's Response

John Mark left them and returned to Jerusalem. - Acts 13:13

After some time Paul said to Barnabas, "Let's go back and visit each city where we previously preached...." Barnabas agreed and wanted to take along John Mark. But Paul disagreed strongly, since John Mark had deserted them in Pamphylia and had not continued with them in their work. Their disagreement was so sharp that they separated. - Acts 15:36-39

Bring Mark with you when you come, for he will be helpful to me in my ministry. - 2 Timothy 4:11

- - - ———— - - -

These verses reveal a conflict met head-on and eventually resolved. God worked in this disagreement to send out two missionary teams instead of one. Later, Mark and Paul resolved their problem and Mark became vital to Paul's ministry. When you're in a conflict, do your best to work things out. If you can't, understand that Christians do not always agree. Problems can be solved by respectfully agreeing to disagree and by letting God work His will.

This Is Promising

Do all that you can to live in peace with everyone. - Romans 12:18

Q

Can I respond to conflict in a way
that pleases God?

God's Response

*Dear friends, never take revenge. Leave that to the righteous anger of
God.... Instead, if your enemies are hungry, feed them. If they are thirsty,
give them something to drink. In doing this, you will heap burning coals of
shame on their heads. Don't let evil conquer you, but conquer evil by doing
good.* - Romans 12:19-21

*Don't repay evil for evil. Don't retaliate.... Instead, pay them back with a
blessing.... Turn away from evil and do good. Search for peace, and work
to maintain it.* - 1 Peter 3:9, 11

How do you resolve conflict? The Bible says to refuse to retaliate.
How can you do that when every part of your nature screams out
for revenge? First, take time out to cool off. Then listen. Perhaps
you have misunderstood or perhaps the person you disagree with
is actually right. In any case, make peace your aim. You don't have
to roll over and be walked on in order to make peace. Actually, you
have to be a strong person to hold your temper and your tongue.
As with exercise, the more you do it, the stronger you will get.

This Is Promising

*God blesses those who work for peace, for they will be called the children of
God.* - Matthew 5:9

Why is it important to confront others
who are doing bad or harmful things?

God's Response

*When Peter came to Antioch, I had to oppose him to his face, for what
he did was very wrong. When he first arrived, he ate with the Gentile
Christians, who were not circumcised. But afterward, when some friends of
James came, Peter wouldn't eat with the Gentiles anymore. He was afraid
of criticism from these people who insisted on the necessity of circumcision.*
- Galatians 2:11-12

Peter was being a hypocrite, so Paul confronted Peter before his
actions could hurt the church. You need to confront a person if
what he or she is doing is self-destructive or hurtful to others. Note
that Paul didn't go behind Peter's back or over his head. Instead, he
went right to Peter. If you are convinced that someone is harming
himself/herself or the church, try the direct approach. If you don't
say something, who will?

This Is Promising

The godly give good advice to their friends; the wicked lead them astray.
- Proverbs 12:26

Q

How should I respond when someone confronts me?

God's Response

This is what our beloved brother Paul also wrote to you with the wisdom God gave him—speaking of these things in all of his letters. Some of his comments are hard to understand, and those who are ignorant and unstable have twisted his letters to mean something quite different, just as they do with other parts of Scripture. And this will result in their destruction. - 2 Peter 3:15-16

Peter had been confronted by Paul (see yesterday's reading). We have no record of his response at that time, but from the verses above, it appears that Peter had great respect for Paul, equating Paul's letters with "the other parts of Scripture." When someone confronts you, take a moment to think and consider the source. Ask God if He sent this person to help you see something in your character that you hadn't seen before. Thank God for people who care enough to speak the truth. Being humble enough to admit when you're wrong is a sign of great strength.

This Is Promising

As iron sharpens iron, a friend sharpens a friend. - Proverbs 27:17

Q Sometimes people make me so angry. How can I deal with my anger?

God's Response

Don't sin by letting anger control you. Don't let the sun go down while you are still angry. - Ephesians 4:26

Get rid of all bitterness, rage, anger, harsh words, and slander, as well as all types of evil behavior. Instead, be kind to each other, tenderhearted, forgiving one another, just as God through Christ has forgiven you.
- Ephesians 4:31-32

Anger can be positive or negative. It can motivate you to right a wrong and to make positive changes. It can also make you lose control and do something harmful or even violent. When you feel anger rising inside, train yourself to step away for a moment to cool off and think. Who is really offended in this situation? Is this about God's honor or your pride? Is it a miscommunication? Allowing bad anger to simmer leaves the door open to many sins. As hard as it sounds, kindness and forgiveness melt anger away. Praying for your enemies, as Jesus taught, makes it impossible to stay angry at them. Learning to bring your emotions under the Holy Spirit's control is part of the process of spiritual maturity.

This Is Promising

Sensible people control their temper; they earn respect by overlooking wrongs. - Proverbs 19:11

Q	What can I do to reduce my angry responses to people?

God's Response

A gentle answer deflects anger, but harsh words make tempers flare.
- Proverbs 15:1

Mockers can get a whole town agitated, but the wise will calm anger.
- Proverbs 29:8

Don't sin by letting anger control you. Think about it overnight and remain silent. - Psalm 4:4

Anger is like mud; you can brush it off much more easily when it's dry. You can reduce your angry responses not by reacting, but by responding. Reacting occurs without thought; responding can happen after you've had a chance to cool off and gain God's perspective. Giving in to anger gives even more power to the source of your anger. Striking back invites the other person to strike back harder. Ask God to help you respond with gentleness and wisdom.

This Is Promising

God called you to do good, even if it means suffering, just as Christ suffered for you. He is your example, and you must follow in His steps.... He did not retaliate when He was insulted, nor threaten revenge when He suffered. He left His case in the hands of God, Who always judges fairly.
- 1 Peter 2:21, 23

Q Where can I find the courage to deal with life's obstacles?

God's Response

The LORD your God ... is with you! - Deuteronomy 20:1

The LORD is my light and my salvation—so why should I be afraid?
- Psalm 27:1

Don't be afraid, for I am with you. Don't be discouraged, for I am your God. I will strengthen you and help you. I will hold you up with My victorious right hand. - Isaiah 41:10

The more convinced you are that you can overcome an obstacle, the bolder you will be in attacking it. If you are convinced that God is going to help you overcome your obstacles, then you will be even more courageous in moving ahead. This conviction that God will help comes mostly from reading and studying God's Word, where you'll discover His desire and power to accomplish great things through you.

This Is Promising

Be strong and very courageous. Be careful to obey all the instructions Moses gave you. Do not deviate from them, turning either to the right or to the left. Then you will be successful in everything you do. - Joshua 1:7

Q Some people at school claim to be atheists. What does that mean?

God's Response

Only fools say in their hearts, "There is no God." - Psalm 14:1

Ever since the world was created, people have seen the earth and sky. Through everything God made, they can clearly see His invisible qualities—His eternal power and divine nature. So they have no excuse for not knowing God. - Romans 1:20

Most importantly, I want to remind you that in the last days scoffers will come, mocking the truth and following their own desires. They will say, "What happened to the promise that Jesus is coming again?" - 2 Peter 3:3-4

Atheists say there is no God. They don't want to recognize God because then they would have to respond to Him and obey His rules. They believe that this life is all there is, so they can live however they please without eternal consequences. But if there is no God, why spend so much time and energy trying to prove He doesn't exist? What we decide about God's existence is literally a choice between life and death. If we decide that He exists, we must then decide how we will respond to His clear message in the Bible.

This Is Promising

His purpose was for the nations to seek after God and perhaps feel their way toward Him and find Him—though He is not far from any one of us.
- Acts 17:27

Q What can I say to an atheist about why I believe in God?

God's Response

That same hour the judgment was fulfilled, and Nebuchadnezzar was driven from human society. He ate grass like a cow.... He lived this way until his hair was as long as eagles' feathers and his nails were like birds' claws. "After this time had passed, I, Nebuchadnezzar, looked up to heaven. My sanity returned, and I praised and worshiped the Most High and honored the One Who lives forever.... He does as He pleases among the angels of heaven and among the people of the earth." - Daniel 4:33-35

- - - ———————— - - -

The best way to talk to an atheist is simply to tell your own spiritual story. Nobody can argue with your experiences. Nebuchadnezzar thought he was God until God stepped in and showed him otherwise. How has God changed your life for the better? That's the story to tell.

This Is Promising

I am doing this so all who see this miracle will understand what it means—that it is the LORD who has done this, the Holy One of Israel Who created it. - Isaiah 41:20

Q

Sometimes I feel really afraid.
What can I do when I am overcome by fear?

God's Response

A leader of the local synagogue, whose name was Jairus, arrived. When he saw Jesus, he fell at His feet, pleading fervently with him. "My little daughter is dying," he said. "Please come and lay Your hands on her; heal her so she can live." … Messengers arrived from the home of Jairus, the leader of the synagogue. They told him, "Your daughter is dead. There's no use troubling the Teacher now." But Jesus overheard them and said to Jairus, "Don't be afraid. Just have faith." - Mark 5:22-23, 35-36

When they saw Him walking on the water, they cried out in terror…. Jesus spoke to them at once. "Don't be afraid," He said. "Take courage! I am here!" - Mark 6:49-50

Why did Jesus tell all these people not to be afraid? He knew that fear would paralyze them. It keeps you from moving out in courage to do the things God wants you to do. It keeps you from trusting God to take care of you. It convinces you that you will fail, that you will let others down, and that God will not help when you need it most. In short, fear consumes you until you can't think straight. When you are frightened, stop and focus on God. Picture Him fighting by your side and your fear will begin to melt away.

This Is Promising

Do not be afraid, for I am with you. - Isaiah 43:5

Q

Is Satan real?

God's Response

This great dragon—the ancient serpent called the devil, or Satan, the one deceiving the whole world—was thrown down to the earth with all his angels. - Revelation 12:9

Jesus was led by the Spirit into the wilderness to be tempted there by the devil. - Matthew 4:1

Humble yourselves before God. Resist the devil, and he will flee from you. - James 4:7

Satan and his demons are fighting even now for your soul. Satan, also called the devil, is a fallen angel who rebelled against God and was thrown out of heaven. Angels who were loyal to Satan were also thrown out; they are called demons. Satan wants to defeat God and rule the world. God allows him to wield a lot of power over the earth for now, because God will not force people to love Him. You must choose between good and evil, between God and Satan. Until you decide whom to follow, Satan will do everything in his power to keep you from following God. After you choose to follow God, Satan will try to sabotage your walk with God. Be aware of this battle for your soul, and determine to stand strong against the evil one. God's great power can always defeat Satan.

This Is Promising

The devil has come down to you in great anger, knowing that he has little time. - Revelation 12:12

Q How powerful is Satan?

God's Response

"All right, do with him as you please," the LORD said to Satan. "But spare his life." - Job 2:6

When Jesus arrived on the other side of the lake, in the region of the Gadarenes, two men who were possessed by demons met him. They lived in a cemetery and were so violent that no one could go through that area. - Matthew 8:28

The Accuser, Satan, was there at the angel's right hand, making accusations against Jeshua. And the LORD said to Satan, "I, the LORD, reject your accusations, Satan. Yes, the LORD, who has chosen Jerusalem, rebukes you." - Zechariah 3:1-2

We make three common mistakes about Satan—we underestimate his power, we overestimate his power, or we ignore him altogether. Satan is very powerful. Only God is more powerful, so if you don't have God in your life, you are in danger of being overwhelmed by Satan's temptations. You can't handle Satan on your own, but Satan is limited by God and can only do what God permits him to do. With Jesus in your heart, Satan cannot control you. Be alert to his daily temptations, and realize that the power of Jesus in your life can render Satan ineffective.

This Is Promising

The devil, who had deceived them, was thrown into the fiery lake of burning sulfur. - Revelation 20:10

Q

What is spiritual warfare?

God's Response

We are not fighting against flesh-and-blood enemies, but against evil rulers and authorities of the unseen world, against mighty powers in this dark world, and against evil spirits in the heavenly places. - Ephesians 6:12

The world offers only a craving for physical pleasure, a craving for everything we see, and pride in our achievements and possessions. These are not from the Father, but are from this world. - 1 John 2:16

Put on all of God's armor so that you will be able to stand firm against all strategies of the devil. - Ephesians 6:11

Satan is alive and well, and his legions of demons are always on the attack. A battle rages in the spiritual realm—you can't see it, but you will experience it if you serve God. You need God's power, not your own, to stand strong and not allow temptations to draw you away. Most of all, since you do not always know or understand the evil that is threatening you, you need God's strength for facing an unknown enemy. Prepare yourself by putting on the armor God gives you to protect you from battle. Read His Word and communicate with Him daily.

This Is Promising

The God of peace will soon crush Satan under your feet. - Romans 16:20

Q

Does spiritual warfare affect me?

God's Response

Stay alert! Watch out for your great enemy, the devil. He prowls around like a roaring lion, looking for someone to devour. Stand firm against him, and be strong in your faith. - 1 Peter 5:8-9

[The devil] was a murderer from the beginning. He has always hated the truth, because there is no truth in him. When he lies, it is consistent with his character; for he is a liar and the father of lies. - John 8:44

· · · ——— · · ·

The purpose of evil is to defy God and wear you down so that you will sin—or at least become useless for God. Be alert at all times. Satan will distort God's Word. He'll make the words of teachers or professors who don't believe in God seem to make sense and he'll try to make you doubt your faith. The battle is on—and your heart is ground zero.

This Is Promising

Don't let anyone capture you with empty philosophies and high-sounding nonsense that come from human thinking and from the spiritual powers of this world, rather than from Christ. - Colossians 2:8

Q

In spiritual warfare, how do I fight back?

God's Response

Take the sword of the Spirit, which is the word of God. - Ephesians 6:17

Humble yourselves before God. Resist the devil, and he will flee from you. - James 4:7

"Get out of here, Satan," Jesus told him. "For the Scriptures say, 'You must worship the LORD your God and serve only Him.' " - Matthew 4:10

Your best offensive weapon is the Word of God. It's odd to think of the Bible as a weapon, but in it, God reveals His plan of attack against everyone and everything that tries to bring you down. It's your battle plan; if you don't read it, you won't know how to fight the battle that literally determines your destiny, here on earth and for eternity. Only by knowing whom you are fighting, where the battle is, and how to defend yourself will you be able to win. It is vital to read God's Word as regularly as possible. This weapon will send Satan running for cover.

This Is Promising

The word of God is alive and powerful. It is sharper than the sharpest two-edged sword, cutting between soul and spirit, between joint and marrow. It exposes our innermost thoughts and desires. - Hebrews 4:12

Q Are demons real?

God's Response

The devil ... was thrown down to the earth with all his angels.
- Revelation 12:9

Jesus rebuked the demon in the boy, and it left him. From that moment the boy was well. - Matthew 17:18

A man possessed by a demon—an evil spirit—began shouting at Jesus.
- Luke 4:33

The demons kept begging Jesus not to send them into the bottomless pit.
- Luke 8:31

Demons are fallen angels who joined Satan in his rebellion against God and are now evil spirits under Satan's control. They help Satan tempt people to sin and have great destructive powers, although they are not able to read your mind and cannot be everywhere at once. Demons are real and active, but Jesus has authority over them and He gave this authority to His followers. Satan and his demons will eventually be thrown into the lake of fire, forever ending their evil work in the world.

This Is Promising
You say you have faith, for you believe that there is one God. Good for you! Even the demons believe this, and they tremble in terror! - James 2:19

Q Do demons and angels really fight?

God's Response

Your request has been heard in heaven. I have come in answer to your prayer. But for twenty-one days the spirit prince of the kingdom of Persia blocked my way. Then Michael, one of the archangels, came to help me, and I left him there with the spirit prince of the kingdom of Persia.
- Daniel 10:12-13

Even Michael, one of the mightiest of the angels, did not dare accuse the devil of blasphemy, but simply said, "The Lord rebuke you!" (This took place when Michael was arguing with the devil about Moses' body.) - Jude 1:9

· · · ——— · · ·

God answered Daniel's prayer by sending an angel to help. Another powerful spiritual being ("the spirit prince of the kingdom of Persia") detained the angel for three weeks, and the two beings fought until a second angel, Michael, came to help. All of this was in response to Daniel's prayer. Be aware that a battle does indeed rage in the spiritual realm. Angels and demons are constantly fighting, and they are fighting over you! Your prayers are heard by God and are a powerful weapon in the battle against Satan.

This Is Promising
I am convinced that nothing can ever separate us from God's love. Neither death nor life, neither angels nor demons. - Romans 8:38

Q There's a group at school who say they are good witches. Is that okay?

God's Response

Household gods give worthless advice, fortune-tellers predict only lies, and interpreters of dreams pronounce falsehoods that give no comfort. So my people are wandering like lost sheep; they are attacked because they have no shepherd. - Zechariah 10:2

Do not practice fortune-telling or witchcraft. - Leviticus 19:26

· · · ——— · · ·

There's no such thing as a good witch. God outlaws all witchcraft—no matter how innocent it may appear—because He is not the source of their power. Witchcraft looks to an authority other than God—Satan. At best, these witches are fakes just having a little fun; at worst, they are in contact with evil spirits and are thus extremely dangerous. Satan is behind the occult. Today, many books, television shows, and games emphasize fortune-telling, séances, and other occult practices. These are not as harmless as they appear to be. They counterfeit God's power in order to look good, but they are rooted in evil and are totally opposed to God.

This Is Promising

Those who practice witchcraft ... their fate is in the fiery lake of burning sulfur. - Revelation 21:8

Horoscopes

Q Is it wrong to read my horoscope every day? Sometimes it's creepy how accurate it is.

God's Response

God made two great lights, the sun and the moon.... He also made the stars. God set these lights in the sky to light the earth. - Genesis 1:16-17

He made all the stars—the Bear and Orion, the Pleiades and the constellations of the southern sky. - Job 9:9

Do not act like other nations, who try to read their future in the stars. - Jeremiah 10:2

Horoscopes are written by the kind of people the prophet Jeremiah warned about, who are trying to read their future in the stars. The truth is that God created the stars and never meant for you to be able to read the future through them. When you want to know something, ask Him, and He will give you the information you need. Horoscopes seem so correct because they're so general that there's little chance of their being wrong. Read the newspaper to find out what happened yesterday. Read the Bible, God's Word, to find out what will happen in the future—God has not been wrong yet.

This Is Promising

My future is in Your hands. - Psalm 31:15

Horror Show

Q

Is it okay to watch horror movies?
Where should I draw the line?

God's Response

Fix your thoughts on what is true, and honorable, and right, and pure, and lovely, and admirable. Think about things that are excellent and worthy of praise. - Philippians 4:8

It is what comes from inside that defiles you. For from within, out of a person's heart, come evil thoughts. - Mark 7:20-21

This is one of those areas where you may or may not be more sensitive than others. You need to draw the line at the place where you feel that what you are putting into your mind is affecting your life. While it may not be a sin to go to a particular movie, take the time to consider how that movie made you feel. What kinds of thoughts did it provoke? The real test is whether watching that movie took you one step closer to God or one step further away. Be very careful. There is plenty of horror in the real world; repeated exposure to horror desensitizes you over time until you no longer see what is wrong with it.

This Is Promising

May the words of my mouth and the meditation of my heart be pleasing to You, O LORD, my rock and my redeemer. - Psalm 19:14

November

Q How can I avoid comparing myself with others?

God's Response

Peter turned around and saw behind them the disciple Jesus loved…. Peter asked Jesus, "What about him, Lord?" Jesus replied, "If I want him to remain alive until I return, what is that to you? As for you, follow Me."
- John 21:20-22

· · · ——————— · · ·

In this profound, loving rebuke, Jesus told the impulsive Peter that he was not to be concerned about God's plans for anyone except himself. God had plans for Peter, and He had plans for John ("the disciple Jesus loved"); He has plans for your Christian friends, and He has plans for you. It is foolish to try to determine whether your hand or your foot is more important—you need both. God created you and every other believer to play a certain role in His Kingdom. Only when you work together will God's Kingdom grow and flourish! Constantly comparing yourself to someone else might cause you to miss what God has for you.

This Is Promising
We are each responsible for our own conduct. - Galatians 6:5

Q

What are the dangers of comparing myself to others?

God's Response

This was their song: "Saul has killed his thousands, and David his ten thousands!" This made Saul very angry. - 1 Samuel 18:7-8

We want to be like the nations around us. - 1 Samuel 8:20

The Pharisee stood by himself and prayed this prayer: "I thank You, God, that I am not a sinner like everyone else. For I don't cheat, I don't sin, and I don't commit adultery. I'm certainly not like that tax collector!" - Luke 18:11

When you compare yourself to others, you take your eyes off Jesus, and this will always cause problems. You may want what others have and become jealous and discontented. You may want to be what others are and miss God's plan for who you are to be. You might end up thinking that you are better than someone else and become arrogant. You might want to do what others are doing and be led into sin. A better plan is just to keep your eyes on Jesus, the perfect standard of comparison.

This Is Promising

Examine yourselves to see if your faith is genuine. Test yourselves.

- 2 Corinthians 13:5

Q

How can I control my thoughts when I start to get jealous of someone?

God's Response

From that time on Saul kept a jealous eye on David.... A tormenting spirit from God overwhelmed Saul. - 1 Samuel 18:9-10

Saul had a spear in his hand, and he suddenly hurled it at David.
- 1 Samuel 18:10-11

Saul was then afraid of David. - 1 Samuel 18:12

Notice the progression of Saul's jealousy. It began with envy that festered and grew until it tormented him. This torment led to uncontrolled rage and finally, to paranoia. Saul's jealousy consumed him to the point that he could think of nothing else and he felt that only murder would solve his problem. He had obviously become completely ineffective for God. This story illustrates the power of jealousy to take over your life unless you take steps to stop it. To stop jealousy in its tracks, you must stop comparing your situation with that of others and instead focus on what God has given to you.

This Is Promising

A peaceful heart leads to a healthy body; jealousy is like cancer in the bones. - Proverbs 14:30

Q

Can I cultivate the discipline of obeying God?

God's Response

Commit yourselves wholeheartedly to these words of Mine. Tie them to your hands and wear them on your forehead as reminders. Teach them to your children. Talk about them when you are at home and when you are on the road, when you are going to bed and when you are getting up. Write them on the doorposts of your house and on your gates.
- Deuteronomy 11:18-20

. . . ——— . . .

For most of us, it is difficult to make obedience a daily habit; we are often tempted to give in to those sins that we enjoy the most. Here are four principles in the discipline of obedience: (1) Focus on Scripture by reading and reciting it daily. (2) Teach Scripture to others to help you apply it to your life. (3) Talk about the Bible and spiritual topics every chance you get. Tell others what God means to you. (4) Keep a spiritual diary or journal, writing down Scripture passages and what you learn from them. If you follow these four principles every day, you will come to love obedience and it will be part of your everyday life.

This Is Promising

Be earnest and disciplined in your prayers. - 1 Peter 4:7

Q I don't like a lot of things about my appearance. Why did God make me this way?

God's Response

You made all the delicate, inner parts of my body and knit me together in my mother's womb. Thank You for making me so wonderfully complex.... You watched me as I was ... woven together in the dark of the womb. You saw me before I was born. Every day of my life was recorded in Your book.
- Psalm 139:13-16

For reasons only God knows, He wants you exactly the way He made you and He has plans for you. Maybe you are a late bloomer and just need to give your body time to mature. Maybe you are just being too hard on yourself and comparing your body to people in magazines and in the movies. What you see there isn't real, and very few people really look that good. Meanwhile, make the most of your assets—develop a fun and positive personality and strong integrity. When you remember that the Master Creator made you, you can walk into any situation with confidence, regardless of your looks.

This Is Promising

Don't be concerned about the outward beauty of fancy hairstyles, expensive jewelry, or beautiful clothes. You should clothe yourselves instead with the beauty that comes from within ... which is so precious to God. - 1 Peter 3:3-4

Q

How do I get beyond someone's appearance and get to know them?

God's Response

Don't judge by his appearance or height.... The LORD doesn't see things the way you see them. People judge by outward appearance, but the LORD looks at the heart. - 1 Samuel 16:7

Charm is deceptive, and beauty does not last; but a [person] who fears the LORD will be greatly praised. - Proverbs 31:30

One of the hardest things to do is to look beyond a person's appearance right into his or her heart. Outward appearances are distracting, whether a person is beautiful or unattractive. Just as you must exercise your body to keep it healthy, you must exercise your mind to keep it in good shape. A healthy mind is smart enough to look beyond physical appearance; it becomes an expert in recognizing inner beauty. This will open up all kinds of potential new relationships. You will be drawn to those who are beautiful on the inside. For those who aren't, you will be better trained to help them do a makeover of their inner selves. When Jesus cleanses us from sin, He makes us beautiful on the inside.

This Is Promising

How can I know all the sins lurking in my heart? Cleanse me from these hidden faults. - Psalm 19:12

Q
Do my thoughts affect my actions?

God's Response

You have heard the commandment that says, "You must not commit adultery." But I say, anyone who even looks at a woman with lust has already committed adultery with her in his heart. - Matthew 5:27-28

Your eye is a lamp that provides light for your body. When your eye is good, your whole body is filled with light. But when your eye is bad, your whole body is filled with darkness. And if the light you think you have is actually darkness, how deep that darkness is! - Matthew 6:22-23

From the heart come evil thoughts, murder, adultery, all sexual immorality, theft, lying, and slander. - Matthew 15:19

The heart is the center of your passions, desires, and beliefs. From your heart come your thoughts and actions. Since all people are born with a sinful nature (Romans 3:23), the heart is naturally corrupt. Therefore, to replace your sinful nature with God's new nature, you must deliberately exclude anything that takes the place of God. He cannot occupy your heart and redeem it if someone or something else already lives there that you are more passionate about. Is God affecting your thoughts and actions, or are you allowing something else to control you?

This Is Promising

The heart of the godly thinks carefully before speaking; the mouth of the wicked overflows with evil words. - Proverbs 15:28

Q

Can my words and actions be beautiful to God?

God's Response

The LORD detests evil plans, but He delights in pure words. - Proverbs 15:26

Timely advice is lovely, like golden apples in a silver basket. - Proverbs 25:11

Let everything you say be good and helpful, so that your words will be an encouragement to those who hear them. - Ephesians 4:29

It's really true—what you spend most of your time thinking about and doing is what you become. When you're tempted to think bad thoughts, train yourself to pray instead. When you're tempted to gossip or say bad words, compliment or encourage someone. When you're tempted to do something that will hurt someone, do something good for them instead. Then you will be known as a person who walks with God, always has something good to say, and is always ready to help. That will make you beautiful in God's sight, and most people will like you as well.

This Is Promising

Let your good deeds shine out for all to see, so that everyone will praise your heavenly Father. - Matthew 5:16

Q How can I encourage others?

God's Response

Barnabas ... means "Son of Encouragement." - Acts 4:36

Barnabas brought him to the apostles and told them how Saul had seen the Lord on the way to Damascus and how the Lord had spoken to Saul. He also told them that Saul had preached boldly in the name of Jesus in Damascus. - Acts 9:27

Saul (Paul) had a terrible reputation with the Christians—after all, he'd been persecuting and killing them. Then he met Jesus and his life (and his name) was changed. It was hard, however, to change people's perception of him, so Barnabas became the bridge between Paul and others. He acted as Paul's sponsor and helped the church leadership to accept that Paul's faith was genuine. Like Barnabas, you can be an encouragement to others by speaking up for them when they've earned your trust and need your support.

This Is Promising

Encourage each other and build each other up. - 1 Thessalonians 5:11

Q

Can I build up other people?

God's Response

Think of ways to motivate one another to acts of love and good works.
- Hebrews 10:24

Love each other with genuine affection, and take delight in honoring each other. - Romans 12:10

We should help others do what is right and build them up in the Lord.
- Romans 15:2

You build others up by finding what is good in them and complimenting them. Don't flatter people just to make them feel good; that isn't honest. But a small word of honest encouragement can often make someone's day. If you have a reputation for integrity, others will know that your words are true.

This Is Promising

Dear brothers and sisters, I close my letter with these last words: Be joyful. Grow to maturity. Encourage each other. Live in harmony and peace. Then the God of love and peace will be with you. - 2 Corinthians 13:11

Q How can I become more thoughtful of others?

God's Response

Be quick to listen, slow to speak, and slow to get angry. - James 1:19

Don't forget to do good and to share with those in need. These are the sacrifices that please God. - Hebrews 13:16

Train yourself to be godly. - 1 Timothy 4:7

- - - - - - - - -

Do you get mad at yourself for missing someone's birthday, not taking part in a missions event, not visiting a friend in the hospital, or not opening the door at the store for a little old lady? Most of us would like to be more thoughtful. A lot of times we think about helping someone but don't do it. Two things can help you be more thoughtful. First, realize that as human beings, we're all pretty self-focused. You're going to need God's help to be aware of others. Ask Him to give you a more thoughtful spirit and the alertness to see opportunities to be of help. Second, train your mind by thinking ahead to things you can do today and during this week to help others. Write these things on your calendar to remind you. As you check them off, you'll develop the great habit of thinking more about others.

This Is Promising

Do to others as you would like them to do to you. - Luke 6:31

Q

Can I let others know I appreciate them?

God's Response

Greet Apelles, a good man whom Christ approves. And give my greetings to the believers from the household of Aristobulus. Greet Herodion, my fellow Jew. Greet the Lord's people from the household of Narcissus. Give my greetings to Tryphena and Tryphosa, the Lord's workers, and to dear Persis, who has worked so hard for the Lord. Greet Rufus, whom the Lord picked out to be His very own; and also his dear mother, who has been a mother to me. - Romans 16:10-13

You can probably still remember the worst thing ever said to you. It has stayed with you, and it still hurts. Can you remember the best thing ever said to you? All of us could stand to hear more words of appreciation and encouragement, so why not start by giving some to others? Paul understood the importance of well-timed words of appreciation. You can let others know that you appreciate them by thanking them and building them up in front of others. Notice what a difference a few words of appreciation can make! What you say to them may be the best words they've ever heard; it may stick with them for a lifetime.

This Is Promising

I have not stopped thanking God for you. I pray for you constantly.
- Ephesians 1:16

Q Why is it important to compliment others?

God's Response

One day Moses said to his brother-in-law, Hobab son of Reuel the Midianite, "We are on our way to the place the LORD promised us, for He said, 'I will give it to you.' Come with us and we will treat you well, for the LORD has promised wonderful blessings for Israel! … You know the places in the wilderness where we should camp. Come, be our guide. If you do, we'll share with you all the blessings the LORD gives us." - Numbers 10:29-32

By complimenting Hobab's desert survival skills, Moses let him know he was needed. People cannot know you appreciate them if you do not tell them they are important to you. Complimenting those who deserve it builds lasting relationships and helps them know how much you value them.

This Is Promising

I am certain that God, Who began the good work within you, will continue His work until it is finally finished on the day when Christ Jesus returns.

- Philippians 1:6

Make It Real

Q How can I be genuine when I compliment someone and not sound like I'm just flattering them?

God's Response

Neighbors lie to each other, speaking with flattering lips and deceitful hearts. May the LORD cut off their flattering lips and silence their boastful tongues. - Psalm 12:2-3

A good person produces good things from the treasury of a good heart, and an evil person produces evil things from the treasury of an evil heart. - Matthew 12:35

The difference between a compliment and flattery is in the motivation behind the words. A compliment is all about the other person, and is designed to build that person up. Flattery is all about you, and is a scheme to get what you want. You don't have to worry about how you come across to others. They'll know whether you mean your words or not. To sound genuine, be genuine.

This Is Promising

… godliness with brotherly affection, and brotherly affection with love for everyone. - 2 Peter 1:7

Q Why should I avoid flattery?

God's Response

To flatter friends is to lay a trap for their feet. - Proverbs 29:5

She seduced him with her pretty speech and enticed him with her flattery. He followed him at once.... He was like a bird flying into a snare, little knowing it would cost him his life. - Proverbs 7:21-23

· · · ——— · · ·

Flattery is lying—saying a lot of sweet stuff to get another person in the mood to give you what you want. Because it is manipulative, flattery is a dangerous trap. When people discover that you have set them up, they may become angry with you. Getting what you want through dishonest means will eventually leave you disillusioned, unfulfilled, and lonely.

This Is Promising

In the end, people appreciate honest criticism far more than flattery.
- Proverbs 28:23

Q

How should I respond when someone compliments me?

God's Response

"The great God was showing the king what will happen in the future. The dream is true, and its meaning is certain." ... The king said to Daniel, "Truly, your God is the greatest of gods, the LORD over kings, a revealer of mysteries, for you have been able to reveal this secret." - Daniel 2:45-47

Nothing in all creation will ever be able to separate us from the love of God that is revealed in Christ Jesus our Lord. - Romans 8:39

Give thanks to the LORD, for He is good! - Psalm 106:1

Daniel received a compliment—he was even being bowed to by the king! However, Daniel let King Nebuchadnezzar know that it was God Who had revealed the meaning of the dream, and then the king praised God. When you are complimented, it's often hard to know how to respond. The best response is simply to say "thank you" and to acknowledge that it is God Who enables you. Then don't forget to pass the compliment on to God with a thankful heart.

This Is Promising

The master said, "Well done, my good and faithful servant. You have been faithful in handling this small amount, so now I will give you many more responsibilities. Let's celebrate together!" - Matthew 25:23

Constructive Criticism

Q How can I give constructive criticism without hurting someone's feelings?

God's Response

When you say they are wicked and should be punished, you are condemning yourself, for you who judge others do these very same things. - Romans 2:1

First get rid of the log in your own eye; then you will see well enough to deal with the speck in your friend's eye. - Matthew 7:5

There is a time and place for healthy criticism, particularly when people are living sinfully or engaging in behavior that is harmful to themselves or others. Criticism can be redemptive if it is truly constructive. Before criticizing, take inventory of your own sins so that you can approach the person with understanding and humility. Then make sure that your words are focused on helping them become all God wants them to be, and not on tearing them down or demeaning them. Constructive criticism should always be given in a spirit of love.

This Is Promising

Some people make cutting remarks, but the words of the wise bring healing. - Proverbs 12:18

On the Hot Seat

Q

How should I respond to criticism?

God's Response

A fool is quick-tempered, but a wise person stays calm when insulted.
- Proverbs 12:16

If you listen to constructive criticism, you will be at home among the wise.
- Proverbs 15:31

Better to be criticized by a wise person than to be praised by a fool!
- Ecclesiastes 7:5

If you are criticized, remain calm and don't lash back. Evaluate whether the criticism is coming from a person with a reputation for wisdom and integrity. Ask yourself if the criticism is meant to heal or to hurt. Is the criticism just and true? Maintain a clear conscience by being honest and trustworthy. This allows you to shrug off criticism you know is unjustified. If criticism is justified, however, you are wise to listen and learn. Perhaps this person has been sent from God to warn you of something you need to know.

This Is Promising

Don't speak evil against each other, dear brothers and sisters. - James 4:11

Q What is the difference between healthy and unhealthy pride?

God's Response

You have been deceived by your own pride because you live in a rock fortress and make your home high in the mountains. - Obadiah 1:3

May I never boast about anything except the cross of our Lord Jesus Christ. - Galatians 6:14

It's okay to feel proud of a job well done when you have honored God in your task. Pride is appropriate when you feel a grateful satisfaction for what God is doing through you. Then your focus is on Him and not on yourself. People with unhealthy pride often think that they know everything, think more highly of themselves than they should, and are blinded to their vulnerability to temptation. Healthy pride is being thankful to God for all He has given—your talents and treasure—that you can use for His glory.

This Is Promising

If you think you are standing strong, be careful not to fall. - 1 Corinthians 10:12

Q Why must I beware of unhealthy pride?

God's Response

Instantly, an angel of the Lord struck Herod with a sickness, because he accepted the people's worship instead of giving the glory to God. So he was consumed with worms and died. - Acts 12:23

When [Uzziah] had become powerful, he also became proud, which led to his downfall. He sinned against the LORD his God by entering the sanctuary of the LORD's Temple and personally burning incense on the incense altar. - 2 Chronicles 26:16

Pride is the main reason for our falling away from God. We become vulnerable to Satan when we believe that we are strong enough to resist his attacks. He loves to prove us wrong. Pride can also creep in when things are going our way and we start to take credit for this. The bottom line on pride boils down to forgetting God. You forget to thank Him, to give Him credit, and to rely on Him. When you reach that point, your pride will lead to a great fall.

This Is Promising

Human pride will be humbled, and human arrogance will be brought down. Only the LORD will be exalted on that day of judgment. - Isaiah 2:17

Q

Can I have enough self-confidence
to do well at school?

God's Response

You have not received a spirit that makes you fearful slaves. Instead, you received God's Spirit when He adopted you as His own children. Now we call Him, "Abba, Father." For His Spirit joins with our spirit to affirm that we are God's children. And since we are His children, we are His heirs. In fact, together with Christ we are heirs of God's glory. But if we are to share His glory, we must also share His suffering. - Romans 8:15-17

You are God's special child. It should give you great confidence to know that God created you for a purpose, has great plans for you, and promises to guide you. See each class, each test, and each assignment as God preparing you for a very special future.

This Is Promising

My heart is confident in You, O God; my heart is confident. No wonder I can sing Your praises! - Psalm 57:7

Giving Thanks

Q Why is it important to thank the Lord?

God's Response

He fell to the ground at Jesus' feet, thanking Him for what He had done. This man was a Samaritan. Jesus asked, "Didn't I heal ten men? Where are the other nine? Has no one returned to give glory to God except this foreigner?" - Luke 17:16-18

Since everything God created is good, we should not reject any of it but receive it with thanks. - 1 Timothy 4:4

Thanking God shows an attitude of gratitude. A thankful heart gives you a positive attitude because it keeps you focused on all God is doing for you. Make giving thanks a part of your prayer time, and thank God for something every day.

This Is Promising

Giving thanks is a sacrifice that truly honors Me. - Psalm 50:23

Q How can I show my thankfulness to the Lord?

God's Response

I will praise You, LORD, with all my heart; I will tell of all the marvelous things You have done. - Psalm 9:1

It is good to give thanks to the LORD, to sing praises to the Most High. It is good to proclaim Your unfailing love in the morning, Your faithfulness in the evening. - Psalm 92:1-2

As I learn Your righteous regulations, I will thank You by living as I should! - Psalm 119:7

There are many ways to show your thankfulness to the Lord— through praise, prayer, singing, worship, giving, obedience, and service. Like you, God also loves to hear a simple "Thank You."

This Is Promising

Give thanks to the LORD and proclaim His greatness. Let the whole world know what He has done. - 1 Chronicles 16:8

Q

What should I thank God for?

God's Response

I will thank the LORD with all my heart as I meet with His godly people. How amazing are the deeds of the LORD! All who delight in Him should ponder them. - Psalm 111:1-2

I praise Your name for Your unfailing love and faithfulness; for Your promises are backed by all the honor of Your name. - Psalm 138:2

Thank God for this gift too wonderful for words! - 2 Corinthians 9:15

. . . —————— . . .

There are so many things to thank God for—salvation, faith, heaven, miracles, food, other believers, family, work, nature, laughter, His unfailing love and faithfulness, His honor, His goodness, His Son ... in fact, you can give thanks for everything good!

This Is Promising

Give thanks for everything to God the Father in the name of our Lord Jesus Christ. - Ephesians 5:20

Q Can I be thankful even in the tough times?

God's Response

Don't worry about anything; instead, pray about everything. Tell God what you need, and thank Him for all He has done. - Philippians 4:6

Be thankful in all circumstances, for this is God's will for you who belong to Christ Jesus. - 1 Thessalonians 5:18

It's hard to be thankful for the tough times, but you can at least be thankful in them. If you can learn to see your troubles as a crucible for strengthening your character and convictions, then you are better able to rise above them and even thank God for the good they are bringing to your life.

This Is Promising

If we are to share [Christ's] glory, we must also share His suffering. Yet what we suffer now is nothing compared to the glory He will reveal to us later. - Romans 8:17-18

Hopelessness

Q What can I do when things seem hopeless?

God's Response

Hannah was in deep anguish, crying bitterly as she prayed to the LORD....
"I have been praying out of great anguish and sorrow." "In that case,"
Eli said, "go in peace! May the God of Israel grant the request you have
asked of Him." "Oh, thank you, sir!" she exclaimed. Then she went back
and began to eat again, and she was no longer sad. - 1 Samuel 1:10, 16-18

Jesus said, "Come to Me, all of you who are weary and carry heavy
burdens, and I will give you rest." - Matthew 11:28

Hannah's situation seemed hopeless, so she took it directly to the
Lord. After she prayed, she left her burden there, went home, ate,
and no longer felt sad. When things seem hopeless, go to God and
let Him have the burden. He wants you to give your burdens to Him
so He can show you how He will help you carry them.

This Is Promising

Why am I discouraged? Why is my heart so sad? I will put my hope in
God! - Psalm 42:11

Q Can I trust in God as my hope?

God's Response

God has given both His promise and His oath. These two things are unchangeable because it is impossible for God to lie. Therefore, we who have fled to Him for refuge can have great confidence as we hold to the hope that lies before us. This hope is a strong and trustworthy anchor for our souls. It leads us through the curtain into God's inner sanctuary.
- Hebrews 6:18-19

The Lord is our source of hope because He tells the truth and keeps His promises. We lose hope when we stop believing that. The Resurrection, the greatest event in history, is the foundation of our hope. Jesus promised that He would rise from the dead, and because He did, you can be assured that every other promise God makes to you will also come true. This changes the way you make choices every day. God has an eternal future planned for you that is far better than anything you can imagine! Live today as though you truly believe that, and see how your perspective changes.

This Is Promising

Without wavering to the hope we affirm, for God can be trusted to keep His promise. - Hebrews 10:23

Q How can I keep hoping when God doesn't seem to act?

God's Response

We were given this hope when we were saved. (If we already have something, we don't need to hope for it.) - Romans 8:24

Faith is the confidence that what we hope for will actually happen; it gives us assurance about things we cannot see. - Hebrews 11:1

Who but God controls the future? Who but God has a home for you that is eternal? Who but God forgives your sins? Who but God gives you a life that lasts forever? The reality is that God is always acting—you just may not always be aware of it. He is always aware, always there, always caring. Keep hoping. God will act at the time and in the way that is best for you.

This Is Promising

O Lord, You alone are my hope. - Psalm 71:5

Q Why does God allow challenges into my life?

God's Response

Dear brothers and sisters, when troubles come your way, consider it an opportunity for great joy. For you know that when your faith is tested, your endurance has a chance to grow. So let it grow, for when your endurance is fully developed, you will be perfect and complete, needing nothing.
- James 1:2-4

Threatening challenges are the very tools God uses to bring you to greater strength and maturity. As you endure these challenges, you receive greater wisdom, integrity, and courage to face whatever comes your way. Somewhere down the road, you will look back and realize how much stronger you became as a result of these challenges, and how God used them to prepare you for the future.

This Is Promising

David continued, "Be strong and courageous, and do the work. Don't be afraid or discouraged, for the LORD God, my God, is with you. He will not fail you or forsake you." - 1 Chronicles 28:20

Q

How do challenges shape my life?

God's Response

My ambition has always been to preach the Good News where the name of Christ has never been heard, rather than where a church has already been started by someone else.... In fact, my visit to you has been delayed so long because I have been preaching in these places. - Romans 15:20-22

Paul's vision for preaching God's good news in different places always drove him to unfamiliar challenges and therefore to greater growth in his relationship with God. Challenges keep you from becoming comfortable and satisfied with the status quo. They require you to follow God's leading into uncharted waters. Let the challenges you face in life give you the faith to try something new and to trust that God is taking you somewhere that you will love where you can make a real difference.

This Is Promising

Commit everything you do to the LORD. Trust Him, and He will help you.
- Psalm 37:5

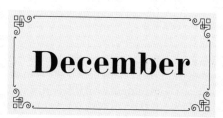

December

Q Can I evaluate advice so I know
if it's good or not?

God's Response

Jeroboam thought to himself, "Unless I am careful, the kingdom will return to the dynasty of David. When these people go to Jerusalem to offer sacrifices at the Temple of the LORD, they will again give their allegiance to King Rehoboam of Judah." ... So on the advice of his counselors, the king made two gold calves. He said to the people, "It is too much trouble for you to worship in Jerusalem. Look, Israel, these are the gods who brought you out of Egypt!" - 1 Kings 12:26-28

You must not make for yourself an idol of any kind.... You must not bow down to them or worship them. - Exodus 20:4-5

It seemed like a good plan to Jeroboam. Problem was, making an idol was clearly against the commands in God's Word. You've got to read the Bible if you want to know what it says. It contains the very words of God, Who wrote them to show you how to experience life in its fullness, and what happens when you ignore or disobey the basic laws of the universe. He created the universe, so He should know how it works! If the advice you're given contradicts the Bible, then it is bad advice. Read the Bible because what it says will literally save your life.

This Is Promising

Oh, the joys of those who do not follow the advice of the wicked. - Psalm 1:1

Giving the Real Scoop

Q Will people listen to my advice?

God's Response

As Samuel grew up, the LORD was with him, and everything Samuel said proved to be reliable. - 1 Samuel 3:19

Fix your thoughts on what is true, and honorable, and right, and pure, and lovely, and admirable. Think about things that are excellent and worthy of praise. - Philippians 4:8

Most people are attracted to godly wisdom. While our ungodly friends may not identify it as God's wisdom, they will want it because it makes so much sense. People listened to Samuel because he had something important to say. This was the case because Samuel had a good adviser—the Lord God. Don't use advice as an excuse to lecture on your point of view. Pray about what you want to say and do your best to provide God's point of view from His Word. Then your words will make all the sense in the world.

This Is Promising

The words of the godly encourage many, but fools are destroyed by their lack of common sense. - Proverbs 10:21

Q

What should I do if I'm experiencing burnout?

God's Response

When David and his men were in the thick of battle, David became weak and exhausted. - 2 Samuel 21:15

I am exhausted and completely crushed. My groans come from an anguished heart. - Psalm 38:8

Moses' father-in-law saw all that Moses was doing for the people, he asked, "What are you really accomplishing here? Why are you trying to do all this alone while everyone stands around you from morning till evening? … You're going to wear yourself out—and the people, too. This job is too heavy a burden for you to handle all by yourself." - Exodus 18:14, 18

If you become unusually weak and exhausted in the middle of doing your work, or if you constantly feel overwhelmed, you may be experiencing burnout. Sometimes you feel burnt out at the end of a project or a great personal victory. When you are stretched in every direction for too long, you lose focus and can't do anything well. You can reach this point quickly when the holidays and finals all seem to crash in on you. To enjoy the spirit of Christmas, you need to pause. Adequate sleep, good nourishment, and asking for help will refresh you so that you can truly enjoy the season.

This Is Promising

He gives power to the weak and strength to the powerless. - Isaiah 40:29

Q I know I can avoid burnout if I set some boundaries for myself. How do I do that?

God's Response

We will boast only about what has happened within the boundaries of the work God has given us, which includes our working with you.
- 2 Corinthians 10:13

Farmers who wait for perfect weather never plant. If they watch every cloud, they never harvest. - Ecclesiastes 11:4

God gives us very clear boundaries for Christian living. These are not meant to keep us from having fun, but to protect us. The same principle applies to our normal, everyday lives. Without boundaries, chaos reigns, we get burned out, and we suffer. To avoid burnout in this busy season, you must set some boundaries. Start by making a list of what you must do and what you'd like to do. Then start scratching things off your list until you feel you will have enough time to enjoy the holiday season. Freeing yourself from the trap of incessant activity requires asking for help and learning to say no, even to worthwhile activities.

This Is Promising

For everything there is a season, a time for every activity under heaven.
- Ecclesiastes 3:1

How will God help me through the weariness of my studies and other activities of this season?

God's Response

I replied, "But my work seems so useless! I have spent my strength for nothing and to no purpose. Yet I leave it all in the LORD's hand; I will trust God for my reward." - Isaiah 49:4

Don't be afraid, for I am with you. Don't be discouraged, for I am your God. I will strengthen you and help you. I will hold you up with My victorious right hand. - Isaiah 41:10

At this point you may feel that many things are worthless—you're tired, you have Christmas shopping to do, money to earn, and studies to complete. Why even bother? God says, "Don't be discouraged." Take one step at a time, and prioritize your day with God's help. You may not be able to finish everything that you want to do, but you can finish all that God wants you to do.

This Is Promising

The Sovereign LORD is my strength! - Habakkuk 3:19

Tithing Time

Q How can I use my time wisely?

God's Response

Be careful how you live. Don't live like fools, but like those who are wise. Make the most of every opportunity in these evil days. Don't act thoughtlessly, but understand what the Lord wants you to do. Don't be drunk with wine, because that will ruin your life. Instead, be filled with the Holy Spirit.
- Ephesians 5:15-18

Give, and you will receive. Your gift will return to you in full—pressed down, shaken together to make room for more, running over, and poured into your lap. The amount you give will determine the amount you get back. - Luke 6:38

It's so easy to waste time. How many times have you said, "I don't even know what I did today"? Here's a suggestion for using your time more wisely. You've heard people tell you to tithe your money (by giving one-tenth of your money to God). Try tithing your time by giving one-tenth of your time to God each day. If you're awake sixteen hours in a day, that's about an hour and a half. Use that time (you can break it up) reading your Bible, praying, going to chapel (if you're at a Christian college), volunteering at church, a soup kitchen, or some other service. Give 10 percent of your time to God, and you will discover that the rest of your time is more wisely spent as well.

This Is Promising

Teach us to realize the brevity of life, so that we may grow in wisdom.
- Psalm 90:12

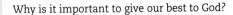

Q

Why is it important to give our best to God?

God's Response

Be sure to give to the LORD the best portions of the gifts given to you.
- Numbers 18:29

Honor the LORD … with the best part of everything you produce. Then He will fill your barns with grain. - Proverbs 3:9-10

God loved the world so much that He gave His one and only Son. - John 3:16

What does it mean to give your best to God? It means giving Him the first part of any income you make. It means giving Him time when you are alert and refreshed, and scheduling time to serve Him instead of just trying to fit Him in somewhere. It means trying your hardest to follow Jesus' example in how you live each day. You don't have to walk around quoting Bible verses all the time, but you should find out what God has called you to do (right now it's to be a student, but someday maybe you will be a carpenter, nurse, or pastor), and go for it with all you've got. Giving your best to God shows that God is first in your life.

This Is Promising

Work willingly at whatever you do, as though you were working for the Lord rather than for people. Remember that the Lord will give you an inheritance as your reward, and that the Master you are serving is Christ.
- Colossians 3:23-24

Q How can waiting make my faith stronger?

God's Response

The LORD your God will drive those nations out ahead of you little by little. You will not clear them away all at once, otherwise the wild animals would multiply too quickly for you. - Deuteronomy 7:22

There is so much more I want to tell you, but you can't bear it now. - John 16:12

When the right time came, God sent His Son. - Galatians 4:4

God often asks you to wait while He leads you along the path of progressive, not immediate, victory. Why? Sometimes this keeps you from the pride that often comes after success. Sometimes it saves you from defeat. And sometimes God makes you wait to prepare you for a special work He has for you. Waiting time is never wasted by God, so don't waste it by being anxious. Serve God as you wait for Him to accomplish the next good thing in your life.

This Is Promising

Be still in the presence of the Lord and wait patiently for Him to act. Don't worry about evil people who prosper or fret about their wicked schemes. - Psalm 37:7

Change

Q With all the changes in my life, how can I keep it all together?

God's Response

LORD, You remain the same forever! Your throne continues from generation to generation. - Lamentations 5:19

Heaven and earth will disappear, but My words will never disappear. - Mark 13:31

God our Father, who created all the lights in the heavens … never changes or casts a shifting shadow. - James 1:17

You are always the same. - Hebrews 1:12

Since change is inevitable in this life, take comfort in the Lord, Who never changes. You can rely on His faithfulness that has not changed from generation to generation, His love that never shifts or dies, His promises that are rock solid, and His salvation that lasts for eternity. Cling to the One Who controls the universe when your world spins out of control.

This Is Promising

Jesus Christ is the same yesterday, today, and forever. - Hebrews 13:8

Just a Little Bit More

Q

Can I find contentment?

God's Response

I have learned how to be content with whatever I have. I know how to live on almost nothing or with everything. I have learned the secret of living in every situation, whether it is with a full stomach or empty, with plenty or little. - Philippians 4:11-12

Contentment is among life's most elusive qualities. The answer to "How much is enough?" always seems to be, "Just a little bit more." The key to Paul's contentment was that he was grateful for everything God had given him rather than envious of what he didn't have. Contentment begins with realizing that we aren't dependent on how much we own. When we realize that there is more to life than accumulating things, everything takes on a new value. Knowing that Jesus gives you strength and help for every situation you face gives you freedom from having to find your security in possessions.

This Is Promising

I can do everything through Christ, Who gives me strength. - Philippians 4:13

Q How do I deny myself and put others first as Jesus did?

God's Response

If you try to hang on to your life, you will lose it. But if you give up your life for My sake and for the sake of the Good News, you will save it. And what do you benefit if you gain the whole world but lose your own soul? Is anything worth more than your soul? If anyone is ashamed of Me and My message in these adulterous and sinful days, the Son of Man will be ashamed of that person when He returns in the glory of His Father with the holy angels. - Mark 8:35-38

To deny yourself doesn't mean that you can't have or enjoy anything; instead, it means that you put Jesus first and others next. Put aside anything that gets in the way of that. Jesus understood that it is fundamentally fulfilling to live in service to others and that living only for yourself will lead to emptiness and disappointment. To have JOY, put Jesus first, Others second, and Yourself last.

This Is Promising

There is no greater love than to lay down one's life for one's friends.
- John 15:13

Q Can I experience God's abundance in my life?

God's Response

How great is the goodness You have stored up for those who fear You. You lavish it on those who come to You for protection, blessing them before the watching world. - Psalm 31:19

Ask, using My name, and you will receive, and you will have abundant joy. - John 16:24

God will generously provide all you need. Then you will always have everything you need and plenty left over to share with others.
- 2 Corinthians 9:8

· · · ——————— · · ·

One of the greatest misconceptions about the Christian life is that God doesn't want you to enjoy it. Satan wants you to believe that God can't wait to punish you for every bad thought and mistake. He wants you to think that you know what is best for yourself. Don't let Satan deceive you. Only God can show you the way to an abundant life. It is in bowing to God's wisdom and in obedience to Him that you will find freedom to live a joyful life.

This Is Promising

My purpose is to give them a rich and satisfying life. - John 10:10

Q

How can I trust God the way Mary did?
Is God really that trustworthy?

God's Response

Mary asked the angel, "But how can this happen? I am a virgin." The angel replied, "The Holy Spirit will come upon you, and the power of the Most High will overshadow you...." Mary responded, "I am the Lord's servant. May everything you have said about me come true." - Luke 1:34-35, 38

How would this young engaged girl explain a sudden pregnancy? She didn't worry about it; instead, she trusted God. She knew she had not had sex, and that she had honored God with her body and her actions. So she knew that God would honor her and take care of her. It's not always easy honoring God, because He may ask you to do some huge task—He asked Mary to give birth to Jesus!—that you feel unfit for. God knows what you can handle because He will walk with you. If you trust Him, He will make sure you accomplish all He asks you to do. What He asks you to do will be more fulfilling than anything you could do on your own.

This Is Promising

When I am afraid, I will put my trust in You. - Psalm 56:3

Why did God become human?
Couldn't He have saved us a different way?

God's Response

Because God's children are human beings—made of flesh and blood—the Son also became flesh and blood. For only as a human being could He die, and only by dying could He break the power of the devil, who had the power of death. - Hebrews 2:14

Without the shedding of blood, there is no forgiveness. - Hebrews 9:22

- - - ———— - - -

Almighty God could have provided all kinds of ways for us to be saved, but He chose a way that demonstrates His great love for us. Jesus became human in order to be like us except for one big difference—He lived His whole human life without sinning once. Imagine that! Because He did not sin, He was the only one who could die for the rest of us, who are all sinners. He took the punishment for sin that we deserved by dying in our place. Then God raised Him from the dead to show that only He—not Satan—has power over life and death. When Jesus promises that we will die once and then be raised to eternal life, we can believe Him. By Jesus' dying and rising from the dead, we are assured that we will do the same if we believe in Him as Lord.

This Is Promising

God showed His great love for us by sending Christ to die for us while we were still sinners. - Romans 5:8

Q

What is meant by Christlikeness?

God's Response

If any of you wants to be My follower, you must turn from your selfish ways, take up your cross daily, and follow Me. - Luke 9:23

I have given you an example to follow. Do as I have done to you. - John 13:15

Jesus Christ is the ultimate example of how to live in a way that pleases God. To follow His example doesn't necessarily mean to be a traveling preacher and do miracles; instead, it means to think His thoughts, show His attitudes, and live as He would live. This is an awesome goal, and since you are not perfect, it will be difficult. The key is not in your ability to be perfect, but in allowing Jesus Christ to live His perfect life through you.

This Is Promising

Follow in His steps. - 1 Peter 2:21

Q How do I become like Christ?

God's Response

All of us who have had that veil removed can see and reflect the glory of the Lord. And the Lord—Who is the Spirit—makes us more and more like Him as we are changed into His glorious image. - 2 Corinthians 3:18

We will speak the truth in love, growing in every way more and more like Christ. - Ephesians 4:15

· · · ——————— · · ·

You can become more and more like Christ by carefully studying how He lived and loved. Then, today and every day, live in such a way that others can see Jesus living in you. Be as accurate a reflection of His truth, love, and mercy as you possibly can.

This Is Promising

I am certain that God, Who began the good work within you, will continue His work until it is finally finished on the day when Christ Jesus returns.
- Philippians 1:6

How can a tiny baby be the mighty God?

God's Response

A Child is born to us, a Son is given to us.... And He will be called: ... Mighty God. - Isaiah 9:6

Suddenly, a fierce storm struck the lake.... [Jesus] got up and rebuked the wind and waves, and suddenly all was calm. The disciples were amazed. "Who is this Man?" they asked. "Even the winds and waves obey Him!" - Matthew 8:24, 26-27

That's why I work and struggle so hard, depending on Christ's mighty power that works within me. - Colossians 1:29

It's hard to picture the baby Jesus as the mighty God, but He was mighty enough to create the world, live a sinless life, heal countless people, calm storms, and conquer death. He is mighty enough to conquer your troubles too!

This Is Promising

Now all glory to God, Who is able, through His mighty power at work within us, to accomplish infinitely more than we might ask or think. - Ephesians 3:20

Q As this year ends, I have some regrets.
How do I deal with them?

God's Response

I focus on this one thing: Forgetting the past and looking forward to what lies ahead, I press on to reach the end of the race and receive the heavenly prize for which God, through Christ Jesus, is calling us. - Philippians 3:13-14

Peter came to Him and asked, "Lord, how often should I forgive someone who sins against me? Seven times?" "No, not seven times," Jesus replied, "but seventy times seven!" - Matthew 18:21-22

This means that anyone who belongs to Christ has become a new person. The old life is gone; a new life has begun! - 2 Corinthians 5:17

As you approach the end of the year, it's natural to look back and reflect on different events. Some memories bring smiles, but others bring regrets. Now is a good time to clean house—that is, to confess to God what needs to be confessed, apologize and make amends to those you have wronged, and then leave the pain behind. Forget the failures of the past and move into the new year with expectation and excitement.

This Is Promising

If we confess our sins to Him, He is faithful and just to forgive us our sins and to cleanse us from all wickedness. - 1 John 1:9

Q

How does Jesus bring peace into my life?

God's Response

Don't let your hearts be troubled. Trust in God, and trust also in Me. There is more than enough room in My Father's home. If this were not so, would I have told you that I am going to prepare a place for you? When everything is ready, I will come and get you, so that you will always be with Me where I am. And you know the way to where I am going. - John 14:1-4

You will keep in perfect peace all who trust in You, all whose thoughts are fixed on You! - Isaiah 26:3

So many things affect peace—chaos, conflict, interruptions, wars, busyness, worry, fear. How can we have peace from all that? On this earth, you can't prevent many of these things from invading your life, but you can have peace—a quiet, unshakeable confidence—about the outcome. How do some people have such peace just before they are martyred for their faith in Jesus? They know where they are going. If you had ten million dollars in the bank, you wouldn't worry about providing for your family if you lost your job. In the same way, if you have banked treasure in heaven, you don't worry about losing your life on earth. Let that assurance keep you from panicking in today's storms. The outcome is certain.

This Is Promising

Here on earth you will have many trials and sorrows. But take heart, because I have overcome the world. - John 16:33

Q What happens when I stay connected to Jesus?

God's Response

I am the true grapevine.... Remain in Me, and I will remain in you. For a branch cannot produce fruit if it is severed from the vine, and you cannot be fruitful unless you remain in Me. Yes, I am the vine; you are the branches. Those who remain in Me, and I in them, will produce much fruit. For apart from Me you can do nothing. - John 15:1, 4-5

When you are connected to Jesus, He turns your simple acts into something profound and purposeful. For example, He turns your simple act of singing into a profound chorus of praise that ministers to an entire congregation. He turns your simple act of placing your tithe in the offering plate into a profound act of mercy that touches the heart of the needy person who receives it. He turns your simple act of telling others your faith story into a profound moment in the heart of a friend who suddenly realizes his or her need for salvation. Stay connected to Jesus and let Him turn your simple acts of service into profound works for the Kingdom of God.

This Is Promising

Now all glory to God, Who is able, through His mighty power at work within us, to accomplish infinitely more than we might ask or think.
- Ephesians 3:20

Q How does God encourage me?

God's Response

No one will be able to stand against you as long as you live. For I will be with you.... I will not fail you or abandon you. - Joshua 1:5

As soon as I pray, You answer me; You encourage me by giving me strength. - Psalm 138:3

"He may have a great army, but they are merely men. We have the Lord our God to help us and to fight our battles for us!" Hezekiah's words greatly encouraged the people. - 2 Chronicles 32:8

· · · ——— · · ·

Joshua's strength and resolve might have weakened over the daunting task of leading all those people into a land of giants. So God prepared him—and the rest of the people—with specific words of encouragement. At times, we long for someone to come beside us, lift us up, and encourage us. How much better if that someone is God! Like Joshua, we don't find courage by looking within or by looking around at the circumstances, but by looking to our sovereign Lord. God encourages us by promising to fight our battles for us.

This Is Promising

May our Lord Jesus Christ Himself and God our Father ... comfort you and strengthen you in every good thing you do and say. - 2 Thessalonians 2:16-17

The Counselor

Q How is Jesus my counselor?

God's Response

A Child is born to us, a Son is given to us.... And He will be called: Wonderful Counselor. - Isaiah 9:6

True wisdom and power are found in God; counsel and understanding are His. - Job 12:13

"Who can know the LORD's thoughts? Who knows enough to teach Him?" But we understand these things, for we have the mind of Christ.
- 1 Corinthians 2:16

If you are fortunate, you have someone in your life on whom you can always depend for advice. You are blessed when that person is not only wise and godly, but loving and caring as well, and always willing to give you as much time as you need. Jesus is such a counselor. He came for the purpose of giving you loving, caring, perfect counsel that will carry you through life and into eternity.

This Is Promising

But I will send you the Advocate—the Spirit of truth. He will come to you from the Father and will testify all about me. - John 15:26

Q Why was Jesus' birth so different?

God's Response

The Savior—has been born today in Bethlehem.... And you will recognize Him by this sign: You will find a baby wrapped snugly in strips of cloth, lying in a manger! - Luke 2:11-12

Remember, dear brothers and sisters, that few of you were wise in the world's eyes or powerful or wealthy when God called you. Instead, God chose things the world considers foolish in order to shame those who think they are wise. And He chose things that are powerless to shame those who are powerful. - 1 Corinthians 1:26-27

· · · ——— · · ·

God often accomplishes His plans in unexpected ways. God used the census of a heathen emperor to bring Joseph and Mary to Bethlehem. Maybe that is also why He chose to have Jesus born in a stable rather than a palace, why He chose tiny Bethlehem rather than the capital (Jerusalem), and why the news of Jesus' birth went first to shepherds rather than to kings. God may have done all this to show that life's greatest treasure—salvation through Jesus— is available to all. It may also show that the lowly and humble are just as important to God as the rich and famous.

This Is Promising

God blesses those who are humble, for they will inherit the whole earth.
- Matthew 5:5

Q

Why did God send His Son into
the world as a baby?

God's Response

*God, with undeserved kindness, declares that we are righteous. He did this
through Christ Jesus when He freed us from the penalty for our sins. For
God presented Jesus as the sacrifice for sin. People are made right with
God when they believe that Jesus sacrificed His life, shedding His blood.
This sacrifice shows that God was being fair when He held back and did
not punish those who sinned in times past. - Romans 3:24-25*

God's mission is to save us for eternity and to show us how to live.
The Incarnation (when the Son of God became a man) means that
God, in the form of a human baby, entered into our world to identify
with our situation, to experience our suffering, and to suffer so that
we could be saved. We can never claim that God doesn't understand
us, because God truly stood where we stand. Refusing to stand aloof
or apart from us, the Lord entered fully into our lives (see Hebrews
2:14-18). As one of us, yet as One Who is also fully divine, He was
able to pay the price for our sins and open the way to eternal life.
He also showed us how to live in surrender and obedience to God
(see John 14:12-14).

This Is Promising

*God loved the world so much that He gave His one and only Son, so that
everyone who believes in Him will not perish but have eternal life. - John 3:16*

Q What should our response be to Jesus?

God's Response

They entered the house and saw the child ... and they bowed down and worshiped Him. - Matthew 2:11

We praise God for the glorious grace He has poured out on us who belong to His dear Son. - Ephesians 1:6

"My Lord and my God!" Thomas exclaimed. - John 20:28

. . . ———— . . .

The astrologers traveled thousands of miles to see the king of the Jews. When they finally found Him, they responded with joy, worship, and gifts. How different from the approach we often take today! We expect God to come looking for us, explain Himself, prove who He is, and give us gifts. Those who are wise still seek Jesus because He is unlike any other person and He was sent for a special purpose. Do you really know who He is? What gift can you give back to Jesus, Who gave His life for you?

This Is Promising

Look! I stand at the door and knock. If you hear My voice and open the door, I will come in, and we will share a meal together as friends. - Revelation 3:20

Q How can I keep Christmas alive all year long?

God's Response

Mary kept all these things in her heart and thought about them often.
- Luke 2:19

Let all that I am praise the LORD; may I never forget the good things He does for me. - Psalm 103:2

Christmas is over, and all the secrets are out. The gifts have been opened, the feast devoured, the songs sung, the joy celebrated. Today is a good day to take some time to reflect, as Mary did more than two thousand years ago, on the events of the big day, on the gifts that were given, and on the love that was bestowed. Store the good times and memories away in your heart so you can think about them and smile over them in the weeks and months ahead. Reflect on the goodness of God, Who gave the best gift of all—His Son. Commit yourself to sharing the story of Christmas all year long.

This Is Promising

We will tell the next generation about the glorious deeds of the LORD, about His power and His mighty wonders. - Psalm 78:4

Q What does it mean to me that
Jesus is coming back?

God's Response

You have every spiritual gift you need as you eagerly wait for the return of our Lord Jesus Christ. He will keep you strong to the end so that you will be free from all blame on the day when our Lord Jesus Christ returns.
- 1 Corinthians 1:7-8

When Jesus returns, all crime, violence, sin, and evil will end. Jesus will restore the earth to its original sinless condition and live among us. He will be king over the earth and the entire universe. Only those who have confessed their allegiance to Jesus will live with Him on this new earth, while those who have not will be eternally separated from Him. Whether or not you like how God has set things up, this is how it is going to be, according to the Bible. It's important to study the Bible carefully to determine Who God is and why He will one day destroy the earth as we know it and begin something new and better. He does it out of love for you, to give you a perfect future. Will you accept what He has done for you, or will you reject Him? The choice is yours.

This Is Promising

He Who is the faithful witness to all these things says, "Yes, I am coming soon!" Amen! Come, Lord Jesus! - Revelation 22:20

Q

How can I plan to finish well next year?

God's Response

The master was full of praise. "Well done, my good and faithful servant. You have been faithful in handling this small amount, so now I will give you many more responsibilities. Let's celebrate together!" - Matthew 25:21

Pay careful attention to your own work, for then you will get the satisfaction of a job well done, and you won't need to compare yourself to anyone else. - Galatians 6:4

Hezekiah encouraged all the Levites regarding the skill they displayed as they served the LORD. - 2 Chronicles 30:22

· · · ———— · · ·

It's almost scary when another year has slipped by. You wonder where it went and how it went by so quickly. That's why it is so important to do your best each day—in your work, in your relationships, in your walk with God, and yes, even in your rest. Be faithful to the responsibilities and the call that God has given you. At year's end, you will have the satisfaction of finishing a job well done, and God will be pleased.

This Is Promising

I am certain that God, Who began the good work within you, will continue His work until it is finally finished on the day when Christ Jesus returns.
- Philippians 1:6

Q What can I do to prepare for the coming year?

God's Response

"I know the plans I have for you," says the LORD. "They are plans for good and not for disaster, to give you a future and a hope." - Jeremiah 29:11

Trust in the LORD with all your heart; do not depend on your own understanding. Seek His will in all you do, and He will show you which path to take. - Proverbs 3:5-6

You can make many plans, but the LORD's purpose will prevail.
- Proverbs 19:21

The LORD says, "I will guide you along the best pathway for your life. I will advise you and watch over you." - Psalm 32:8

God already knows what the next year will hold for you. He has some great plans for you. He will advise you as you go and watch over you along the way. When you have asked for God's guidance and direction, you can move forward with confidence, knowing that His purpose and work for you will get done.

This Is Promising

We know that God causes everything to work together for the good of those who love God and are called according to His purpose for them.
- Romans 8:28

Q

How can I ensure that I will be better off a year from now?

God's Response

He died for everyone so that those who receive His new life will no longer live for themselves. Instead, they will live for Christ, Who died and was raised for them. - 2 Corinthians 5:15

Let the Holy Spirit guide your lives. Then you won't be doing what your sinful nature craves. - Galatians 5:16

Look at those who are honest and good, for a wonderful future awaits those who love peace. - Psalm 37:37

· · · ———— · · ·

There's a whole new year just around the corner. It's a fresh start, with no mistakes made yet. In a sense, this is the chance to become a new person. In the year ahead, commit to growing every day in your relationship with the Lord, even just a little bit. Ask the Holy Spirit to change you, day by day, into all God wants you to be, and a year from now, you will be a better person.

This Is Promising

Anyone who belongs to Christ has become a new person. The old life is gone; a new life has begun! - 2 Corinthians 5:17

Q

What should I stop doing and what should I start doing in order to end this year well and begin the new year well?

God's Response

I am the Alpha and the Omega—the Beginning and the End. To all who are thirsty I will give freely from the springs of the water of life! - Revelation 21:6

·· ·· ———— ·· ··

Stop looking back with regret. Stop thinking you can't overcome a bad habit or addiction. Stop thinking God doesn't care. Stop blaming yourself or others. Stop doing what you know you should not do. Stop doing too much. Stop doing too little. Start each day with God in prayer and Bible reading. Start showing more grace and forgiveness. Start a good new habit. Start obeying God's Word more. Start repairing hurt relationships. Start trusting God to show up in your life every day. This is a good time to commit to stopping and starting and to remembering that God is the one constant that will never change all year. He loves you and will always be at your side. May God bless you on your continuing adventure with Him in the coming year.

This Is Promising

May the LORD bless you and protect you. May the LORD smile on you and be gracious to you. May the LORD show you His favor and give you His peace. - Numbers 6:24-26

Index

—— **R** ——